FACE to FACE

Knowing God beyond Our Shame

FR. STEPHEN FREEMAN

ANCIENT FAITH PUBLISHING   CHESTERTON, INDIANA

Face to Face: Knowing God beyond Our Shame
Copyright © 2023 Stephen Freeman

Published by:
Ancient Faith Publishing
A Division of Ancient Faith Ministries
P.O. Box 748
Chesterton, IN 46304

Unless otherwise noted, Scripture quotations are taken from the New
King James Version, © 1979, 1980, 1982 by Thomas Nelson, Inc. Used by
permission.

ISBN: 978-1-955890-32-8

Library of Congress Control Number: 2022949422

For my family, living and departed

Contents

Introduction

*You cannot know God,
but you have to know Him to know that.*
—FR. THOMAS HOPKO

MY FIRST ENCOUNTER WITH Fr. Thomas Hopko was marked by shame. I was visiting St. Vladimir's Seminary one summer after my family and I had been received into the Orthodox Church. I had become familiar with his work through his writings and recordings. Indeed, I was a bit star-struck as I saw him standing with a couple of priests, engaged in conversation. I approached and found myself tongue-tied and stammering for words of greeting and introduction. The conversation was brief and did nothing to ease my discomfort. I did not know it at the time, but that discomfort was a symptom of much deeper things in my life.

This short encounter with shame was a minor thing in itself, little more than an uncomfortable moment of social awkwardness. It is an example of many similar occasions in our lives—some minor, some devastating and paralyzing. Shame is rarely absent from our lives. Described as the "master emotion," it accompanies us and shapes our social interactions, both for good and for ill.[1] Shame also colors our inner lives, dancing around the experience of identity and our ability to see and understand ourselves. If Hopko is right (and I think he is) that "we cannot know God" but we "have to know Him to know that," it is also true that we cannot know ourselves until we know the unknowable God. Created in His image and likeness, we are irreducibly bound to the knowledge of God in the journey toward our true selves.

The day I stood on the St. Vladimir's campus, awash in my own embarrassment and awkwardness, shame was revealing both myself and God in a waterfall of knowledge that I did not know how to receive. If anything, shame was a most unwelcome companion, incompatible with any possible good outcome. Nevertheless, shame is unavoidable—an inherent part of our lives. It is not necessarily a product of sin, nor is it something that needs to be eliminated from our existence. The Book of Ecclesiasticus (also known as the Wisdom of Sirach) offers this observation: "For there is a shame that brings sin, and there is a shame which is glory and grace" (4:21 OSB).

Shame has a healthy and natural role in our lives that, like all things, can be subject to perversion and abuse. Its abuse is extremely common, and the pain associated with it often gives

---

1 "Shame plays a central role in regulating the expression, and indeed, the awareness of all of our other emotions. Anger, fear, grief, and love, for example, are not likely to be expressed outwardly to the degree that one is ashamed of them. One can be so ashamed of one's emotions that they can be repressed almost completely, to the point that only unusual circumstances will allow them to come to awareness. In Western societies, shame is almost completely repressed and hidden, because one would be embarrassed that one was in a state of grief, fear, anger, or even embarrassment." Scheff and Retzinger, "Shame as the Master Emotion of Everyday Life," *Journal of Mundane Behavior*, January 2000.

it a very negative caste. For this reason, shame is frequently misunderstood or ignored. My personal experience has been that, although I knew something of a textbook definition for shame, I had no idea how pervasive it was in my own life, in the lives of others, or in the culture at large. About ten years ago, a range of personal issues came together for me that forced me to see what I had not seen before and to understand the nature of the invisible forces in my life and personality. The result has been an opening into a realm of theology that is often neglected and overlooked.

As I have made my own progress in working with shame, I have written and shared various insights. I have found that my own experience echoes what is common to us all, for good and for ill. My study has taught me to hear things I did not hear before, particularly as a confessor, and to understand many of the mechanisms in our inner life that often remain opaque. The Tradition of the Faith is no stranger to this topic, I found, though I had to mine the resources with a careful eye and frequently translate them into terms that could more easily be communicated and explained.

I have also spent time in conversation with clinical specialists who work with toxic shame and other related psychological issues. Those conversations have taken me into a study of modern clinical research. My reading and listening have revealed that little has changed over time in the phenomenon of shame, other than how our culture treats it (and avoids it). Some have observed that modern America is a shame-bound culture in which the topic of shame itself is often taboo. Much of the relevant popular writing is found within the self-help industry, which can be both useful and frustrating. Shame is often a public or relational reality, and its treatment requires assistance. Reading a book is not sufficient.

In saying that, I'll quickly state that, whatever usefulness might be found in this book, it will be insufficient for our greater needs. Orthodox Christianity is not a private understanding of the world; it is found in the context of the Church, in her sacraments and in the lives of her people. When I speak of the Tradition of the Church, this is not merely an exercise in recovering some past experience but an effort to draw on the present life of the Orthodox community, which in its depths is formed and shaped by that Tradition.

In contemporary Orthodoxy, I have been particularly indebted to the work and writings of St. Sophrony of the Holy Mountain, as well as those of his disciple, Archimandrite Zacharias of Essex, with whom I was privileged to discuss this topic in some depth. I would describe much of what I am offering in this book as an exploration and expansion of St. Sophrony's teaching. He made the "bearing of a little shame" a key part of the spiritual life of his disciples and taught the world that the "way down is the way up." To a great extent, his language is centered in the word *humility* and the practice of that virtue. We will see as we go along that humility is the acceptance of *healthy* shame in a manner that allows us to see the truth of ourselves as well as the truth of God.

The journey (the way down as the way up) of the spiritual life is the pursuit of the knowledge of God. It inherently includes the knowledge of ourselves, both as we are at present, as we have been wounded, as we are healed, and, finally, as we are in wholeness. Saint Paul connects these experiences in his description of beholding Christ: "But we all, with unveiled face, beholding as in a mirror the glory of the Lord, are being transformed into the same image from glory to glory, just as by the Spirit of the Lord" (2 Cor. 3:18).

The process of understanding shame and slowly making our way through that difficult emotional territory can easily be described as a progressive unveiling of our face. Many people labor with a deformed concept of God, garnered from many sources, just as they labor with a painful and deformed concept of the self, taught and nurtured by a broken culture and often, sadly, by those who are closest to them. The result is a "God" who is not worthy of the word "glory," offered by toxic ministers who are themselves bound by an unidentified and unattended shame. The result is a "shame that brings sin." The path described for us in the Orthodox Tradition, exemplified in the teaching of St. Sophrony and others, is one of "glory and grace."

A theme of shame and its healing runs from Genesis through Revelation. It is often overlooked, as later theological schemes have muted its presence. For example, it became clear to me, listening to the texts of the Holy Week services, that they are dominated by the experience of shame rather than pain. "I did not hide My face from shame and spitting," Isaiah says of the suffering Messiah (50:6). Working through those theological themes adds a richness to our gospel understanding, uniting both the pastoral and the dogmatic in a single theme of healing and redemption.

What Is Shame?

SHAME HAS MANY ASPECTS. IT can be described in emotional, psychological, social, religious, or even political terms. My approach to the topic covers several areas. A primary concern is its place within theology. Does God create shame? Does our Faith require shame of us? What place does shame hold in the life and work of Christ? How do we speak about shame in a manner that is consistent with Orthodox teaching? At the same time, I have an equal concern for the place of shame in an individual's life. The purpose of the Orthodox Faith is not to grind us into the dust, much less to manipulate the vulnerabilities of shame in order to make us compliant and morally acceptable. Whatever the place of shame is in our lives, it is a phenomenon that should be understood in a manner consistent with the love of God.

Shame can be *healthy* or it can be *toxic. Healthy shame* describes the emotional experience of boundaries. It gives signals of vulnerability, nakedness, a desire to hide or protect oneself, or a sense of not-belonging and exposure. These responses can be described as "healthy" in that they are necessary for our well-being. Just as the sense of touch can warn us about the presence of heat, so healthy shame warns us of emotional and social dangers. It gives us vital information.

Toxic shame describes the experience of shame gone wild. Rather than being an emotional signal of a boundary, toxic shame is the result of *shame as an identity.* Such shame is incorporated into the person we experience ourselves to be. As such, it distorts who we are and becomes a foundation for emotional sickness and destructive behaviors. Toxic shame is generally a

result of trauma and abuse, both of which magnify the normative experience of healthy shame into a relentless identity that
begins to smother our ability to manage shameful feelings.[2]

I have adhered to the use of the terms *healthy shame* and
toxic shame throughout this book for the simple reason that the
mechanism beneath both is the same. These forms of shame
differ in the ways that mechanism is triggered and in the emotional contexts that surround them. I have also chosen to use
the term *shame* in both contexts in order to be faithful to the
Tradition (as illustrated in the double meaning in the verse
from Ecclesiasticus quoted above). Later we will hear phrases
such as "healing shame by shame" (St. John of the Ladder).
Such statements can only be understood by using the single
term and differentiating between what is healthy and what is
toxic. I hope this will not be confusing to readers, and I empha-
size here at the outset that one should expect to see this double
meaning.

My own early experience of toxic shame was accompanied
by an anxiety/panic disorder (not at all uncommon). That
debilitating condition dogged my life from my late teen years
until my late fifties. It eventually drove me into discovering
the nature of my shame and the pathway out of it. Living with
anxiety and panic, I learned to pay a great deal of attention
to my body as well as my mind. A panic attack is, essentially,

---

2   See John Bradshaw, *Healing the Shame that Binds You* (Deerfield Beach, FL:
    Health Communications, Inc., rev. ed., 2005), xvii. These terms are used fairly
    consistently in a wide range of clinical writings. I am particularly indebted
    to the work of Bradshaw, as well as that of Silvan Tomkins and Gershan
    Kaufman, both of whom did studies foundational for Bradshaw's popular
    work. Their writings have held up well through the years and remain reliable
    sources for thinking about shame issues.

nothing more than an adrenaline storm. It can be triggered by any number of things: thoughts, situations, memories, and so forth. Nevertheless, underneath everything, the attack is not about thoughts. It is utterly physical. It can be measured and its symptoms charted.

In the early years of my experience with this disorder, no one explained this to me. That lack of knowledge led me a merry chase as I sought to control my thoughts and soothe my emotions, while spending useless hours imagining what deep forces were driving me crazy. When I later discovered the deeply physical nature of an adrenaline storm, it helped. This knowledge did not remove the storm, but it allowed me to reframe the problem. I began to view a panic attack as similar to pain in my arm caused by an injury. It was not a symptom of insanity but simply the experience of what the brain and body feel like when they are bathed with adrenaline. Famously, you feel like either running away or fighting back ("fight or flight syndrome"). That seemed ever so much more manageable than simply being out of my mind.

That realization taught me to value the physical basis of our thoughts and experiences. It does not utterly explain them, but it can provide a much more solid foundation for thinking about what is taking place inside than can wandering around solely in the world of thoughts. Those questions led me to read clinical research on the neurobiological basis of the experience of shame. This approach does not fully explain shame in the sense of encompassing the whole of the experience. However, it is a worthwhile side trip for understanding the full nature of this master emotion.

Orthodox spiritual practices have a deeply physical side. We fast from certain foods, perform prostrations, cross ourselves, and repeatedly encounter Christ in the sacramental forms of sanctified bread, wine, oil, and water. We are not angels, members of the "bodiless hosts." Rather, we are, as a quotation often attributed to St. Gregory of Nyssa says, "mud that has been commanded to become god." Fulfilling this commandment requires that we get our hands muddy with the knowledge of how our body works. Thus, exploring the science of shame is not a detour into secular explanations. Rather, it is taking a deep dive into shame itself, in its *human* form, in order to understand the full nature of our experience.

Over the past ten years, as I have done the research and exploration that now takes the form of this book, the topic of shame has accompanied everything I've done. Whether I'm writing theology, preparing sermons, or reflecting on current events, the question of shame has never departed from my awareness. What has become increasingly clear to me is the all-pervasive presence of shame in our culture. It has made me aware of the language of shame in the marketplace, in the voting booth, on social media, and in the inner voices that haunt our daily lives. Some of the chapters in this book will seek to expose that language. The Orthodox way of life with its path of transformation is frequently out of step with the passions that shape our public narrative. In many ways, the American dream is little more than an effort to escape the shame imagery of our culture through the artifice of success. The dream enthrones shame as the arbiter of our lives.

As I conclude this introduction, I want to pause and thank

my partners in the many conversations that have helped give shape to this work. In my blog writing, I have been assisted by probing questions and insightful comments from those who take time to read and respond. I have equally been assisted by those whom I have met at various retreats and conferences where I have spoken over the past decade. More than anything, the openness and vulnerability of many people have been a constant encouragement to get on with this work. My daily companion and closest spiritual friend is my beloved wife. Her steadfastness and unconditional love have been food for my soul. Shame requires love and acceptance in order to be healed. We cannot make that journey alone. God has given me just that sort of help at every step of the way.

I pray you find this book of use and ask your prayers for others.

CHAPTER ONE

Naked and Ashamed

I WAS STANDING NAKED on Main Street in Kampsville, Illinois. The summer was not turning out as I had imagined. I'd enrolled in a summer archaeology program through Northwestern University. There was a dig outside Kampsville, serving to teach the various skills that make up that field of study. The town, repeatedly flooded by the Illinois River, had been bought up by Northwestern to house its school. Various labs and libraries lined Main Street. Student housing, though, was extremely makeshift. I was staying in an abandoned farmhouse outside town, without running water or indoor facilities. I recall the outdoor privy also being the home of a rather large wasp nest. Shower facilities had been constructed on Main Street.

One afternoon, I found time in my schedule to grab a shower. There were probably three others in the building. In the middle of my shower, I noticed a strange smell and began to have difficulty breathing. Someone cleaning in the shower area had accidentally mixed two cleaning liquids, one that was chlorine-based and one that was ammonia-based. The mixture releases chlorine gas, which irritates and burns the bronchial tract. Exposure is potentially fatal. Coughing and sputtering, those of us in the showers staggered out of the building onto the street. Something about the experience felt like a metaphor: I was naked, alone, exposed, disoriented. I withdrew from the school a week later.

All of us have had dreams in which we find ourselves naked or exposed in a public setting. Generally, those dreams are "shame dreams," unconscious symbols of an inner exposure we feel in various situations. Unwanted exposure is a classic trigger for feelings of shame. Such triggers can be physical, emotional, or related to any setting in which we feel vulnerable and unsafe. Our bodies and minds signal the need to hide (literally or figuratively). That very feeling is related to the human experience in its very beginning.

The story of humanity as told in the early chapters of Genesis unfolds in the context of nakedness. The man and the woman begin in a state of paradisiacal innocence. Nothing describes this better than the simple phrase, "And they were both naked, the man and his wife, and were not ashamed" (Gen. 2:25). Shame is experienced as a break in communion. As will be described in later chapters, our bodies and minds undergo a disruption in the presence of shame. When communion is interrupted, anything is possible. We have no assurance of how things around us will unfold, nor of our own selves and our ability to cope. We experience all this in a moment, not as a train of rational thought but as a response to our brokenness.

The Genesis story begins with communion. Nothing comes between the man and the woman. They are in a world of safety.

God Himself is described as walking in the Garden "in the cool of the day" (Gen. 3:8). However, the nakedness that perfectly images the communion of paradise is transformed when the man and the woman transgress the commandment they have been given. Hearing God walking in the Garden, they hide. In their transgression, we are told, "The eyes of both of them were opened, and they knew that they were naked; and they sewed fig leaves together and made themselves coverings" (Gen. 3:7).

When confronted by God, Adam explains his behavior: "I heard Your voice in the garden, and I was afraid because I was naked; and I hid myself" (Gen. 3:10). The quiet communion of paradise has been interrupted by fear and shame. Nakedness has a new meaning.

This simple account contains no in-depth analysis or speculation, but its richness has lasted through millennia. Its continuing power lies in the fact that it captures a human experience that has remained unchanged. Our own lives move from the innocent communion of our infancy into the messiness of shaming encounters with the world around us as we grow and seek to find a place of safety in which to flourish. That movement into the world is itself something of a parallel to the experience that marks our own many falls. Finding themselves naked and ashamed, the man and the woman try to clothe themselves with fig leaves. Finding ourselves naked and ashamed, we fashion false identities and various strategies of behavior in which to hide. If shame describes "how I feel about who I am," then our various efforts to hide ourselves can be seen as attempts to create a satisfactory protective identity.

It is worth noting, as an aside, that the Genesis account is not the story of how human beings became "evil." Terrible distortions have plagued theology across the centuries, particularly those that view humanity as fundamentally flawed at its very core. Some of the darkest regimes in history have subscribed to this view and left a disturbing legacy of violence and abuse as they sought to control and manage a population viewed as inherently evil.

This distortion is not part of the Tradition of Eastern Christianity. Indeed, Adam and Eve are numbered among the saints and remembered each year before Christmas in the feast of the ancestors of Christ. The role of shame in the Genesis account allows us to see more clearly the dynamic of what is taking place and, subsequently, the dynamic that will mark our healing and reconciliation with God.

The actions of the man and the woman brought about consequences. They broke communion with God. That communion is life itself. God's warning to them had been that breaking His commandment (not to eat of the fruit of the Tree of the Knowledge of Good and Evil) would result in death. This is not a threat. God does not say to them, "If you eat of this fruit, I will kill you." The point is not punishment. The commandment represents the boundary that defines their relationship with God, their communion. To step outside that communion is to step into death.[3]

This death can be understood as describing our physical mortality. However, that final breakdown in communion, the separation of soul and body, is only the last stage of a death

---

3 This dynamic is developed in depth by St. Athanasius in his classic work *On the Incarnation.*

process that we experience day in and day out in our lives in the ruptures of communion that surround us. Those ruptures are not experienced as death, per se, but as occasions of shame, of alienation from God, from others, and from ourselves.

The same is true of the man and the woman in Genesis. God describes for them various elements of their alienation. The ground will not cooperate with them as it had in the Garden. There will be enmity between the two of them. In their offspring, Cain and Abel, we see the first tragic instance of murder, an act in which shame passes over into envy and destroys its antagonist.

An easily overlooked statement in the Genesis story plays an important role in the thoughts of some of the early Church Fathers: "Also for Adam and his wife the Lord God made tunics of skin, and clothed them" (Gen. 3:21). If we read the story with an eye to the dynamic of nakedness and shame, we can see that this is a key verse. The couple is not sent forth in their self-made fig-leaf outfits. Instead, something more enduring and stable is given them by God Himself.

Early interpretations of these garments of skin were wide-ranging. A primary concern was to guard against the gnostic notion that the phrase described our mortal, physical bodies. Human beings are not spirits who fell into material creation.[4]

Perhaps the most helpful way to understand this provisional covering given by God to humanity can be found in the anaphora of the Divine Liturgy of St. Basil:

---

4   Panayiotis Nellas has an interesting discussion of these treatments in his *Deification in Christ* (Crestwood, NY: St. Vladimir's Seminary Press, 1987), 43ff.

But when man disobeyed You, the true God Who had created him, and was misled by the deception of the serpent, he became subject to death through his own transgressions. In Your righteous judgment, O God, You expelled him from paradise into this world, returning him to the earth from which he was taken, yet providing for him the salvation of regeneration in Your Christ Himself. For You, O good One, did not desert forever Your creature whom You had made. Nor did You forget the work of Your hands, but through the tender compassion of Your mercy, You visited him in various ways: You sent prophets. You performed mighty works by Your saints who in every generation were well-pleasing to You. You spoke to us by the mouth of Your servants, the prophets, who foretold to us the salvation which was to come. You gave us the law as a help. You appointed angels as guardians.

In "visiting us in various ways," God provides protection from the nakedness of our mortality and shame. He gave us prophets. He performed mighty works. He gave us the law. He appointed angels as guardians. All these "garments" provide something of a covering. This can be seen particularly in the healthy function of the law.

If we were cast into the world and left entirely to our own inventiveness, every encounter would be as if it were our first. Without some sort of protection, we could not bear the nakedness of our unformed and ill-formed identity. Life would be nothing but struggle and violence, unmitigated alienation, and loss of communion.

As it is, the structures that surround us, whether formally created by the God-inspired law or simply appearing as a distant echo in the mores of contemporary society, give some protective guidelines for our self-understanding and negotiation with the world. No human culture is perfect or completely sufficient for this task. Nonetheless, it is easier to bear our daily existence when we are clothed in the garments of our culture. Language, customs, elements of acceptable behavior all play a part in supporting the life we live. They do not and cannot reveal to us the depths of the soul. However, they can allow us to live some measure of a mortal life in which those depths can be discovered.

The theme of being clothed by God does not end with the Genesis account. It figures prominently in the laws surrounding the temple and the priesthood of the Old Testament. In those images is something of a preview of the covering yet to come that is celebrated in the New Testament. The Psalmist offers an example. Speaking of Zion and the temple, God says:

This is My resting place forever;
Here I will dwell, for I have desired it.
I will abundantly bless her provision;
I will satisfy her poor with bread.
I will also clothe her priests with salvation,
And her saints shall shout aloud for joy.
(Psalm 132:14–16, emphasis added)

The vestments of the priest are not described in terms of cloth and decoration as they are in Leviticus. Instead, they are now the clothing "of salvation." Saint Paul describes the Christian as being clothed with "righteousness and holiness" (Eph. 4:24). Indeed, at every baptism, we traditionally clothe the newly baptized in white garments, singing, "Grant unto me a robe of light." Then we lead the newly clothed three times around the font, singing, "As many as have been baptized into Christ have put on Christ. Alleluia!"

Saint Paul draws on this same imagery when he describes our resurrection:

> For we know that if our earthly house, *this* tent, is destroyed, we have a building from God, a house not made with hands, eternal in the heavens. For in this we groan, earnestly desiring to be clothed with our habitation which is from heaven, if indeed, having been clothed, we shall not be found naked. For we who are *in this* tent groan, being burdened, not because we want to be unclothed, but further clothed, that mortality may be swallowed up by life. Now He who has prepared us for this very thing *is* God, who also has given us the Spirit as a guarantee. (2 Cor. 5:1–5)

Not only does he see our resurrection as a clothing of our mortal nakedness, he sees the present life in the Spirit as a foretaste and guarantee of that which is to come.

This same use of the imagery from Genesis can be applied to the dynamics of our daily lives. The author of the Macarian Homilies sees these external actions and stories also as illustrations of the mysteries of the human heart.[5] Long before we confront the nakedness of our mortality, we inwardly confront the daily nakedness of our broken communion, the pain of shame that afflicts so many of our interactions.

The inmost heart is a deep battleground and the sanctuary of the soul's true existence:

> The heart itself is but a small vessel, yet there also are dragons and there are lions; there are poisonous beasts and all the treasures of evil . . . there is also God, also the angels, the life and the kingdom, the light and the Apostles, the treasures of grace—there are all things. (H.43.7)[6]

This is the perspective that will direct the considerations in this book. There is within us the very image of God: "life and the kingdom . . . the treasures of grace." If shame is part of our answer to the question, "How do I feel about who I am?" this path reminds us that the truth of who I am is not found on the surface. Who I am is not to be mistaken for the "garments of skin"—the various strategies, identities, and designs with which we seek to clothe ourselves. The deepest mode of the spiritual life is one that searches for God, that asks, seeks, and knocks, in order to find the Kingdom. That is a search that takes us beneath layers of shame, beneath our false identities,

---

5   The fifty homilies attributed to St. Macarius were, it seems, written by an anonymous author in the fourth century. They give evidence of a strong Syrian influence. Their emphasis was on the inner struggle of the Christian. These homilies influenced a number of later writers, including St. Diodochus of Photike and St. Isaac of Syria.

6   *Pseudo-Macarius: The Fifty Spiritual Homilies and the Great Letter*, trans. George Maloney (New York: Paulist Press, 1992), 221–22.

into the very place where the image of God and the true self reside. This is a difficult journey.

The Soul Is a Temple

ADOLESCENTS ARE ILL EQUIPPED FOR the difficult journey of the inner life. They have so little experience to draw on; so much is simply unknown. We instinctively protect children and recognize that their innocence is a fragile thing. The Macarian Homilies explore the inner world, the soul, as a reflection of the temple. I have found this imagery to be useful in thinking about the dynamics of shame within us.

The ancient temple in Jerusalem was divided into various sections that became increasingly holy and restricted as one went further in. It is a commonplace that traditional Christian churches came to be structured in the same pattern. They have a narthex, a nave, and an altar area or sanctuary. The narthex is the most public space. It is an area of initial arrival, of possible greetings, and of preparation to enter into the holy space of the nave. The nave is the central space of worship, where the family of God gathers. In early church practice, those who were not yet baptized were dismissed from this area just before the reciting of the Creed. Only those who had been initiated into the mysteries of the Church remained. The altar was reserved for those few who had been set aside as priests, deacons, or servers.

The human being has a similar pattern. We have a public face, the self whom everyone sees, the face with which we greet and encounter the world. It is the least intimate part of our life, largely devoid of secrets. It is significant that this self is the part of us that is most formally clothed. It is what we show the world and, perhaps, the part we wear as a shield, protecting us from prying eyes.

We have a place beneath all this that is more intimate. It is, I think, the place where friendship and family reside. Those who know us are the primary ones we encounter within this space. Here is an increased vulnerability and a greater risk of shame. Our friends and family have far more ability to inflict shame within that space. That is why we are careful about whom we admit into such a relationship.

Finally, we have an inmost region that corresponds to the Holy of Holies. This is the part of us in which and through which we encounter God, in the deepest realms of our own self. This is generally a place we rarely enter. It holds mysteries of both God and self that become known only with labor and patience.

All of this functions well when it is understood and properly governed. The structures of most cultures (the "garments of skin") provide norms and rules that restrict access to the deeper realms of the soul. In a polite society, we can say that certain actions and inquiries are inappropriate, meaning they attempt entry into a place where they are not permitted. For example, such norms say that children should be shielded from adult knowledge. If any sexual education takes place, we consider at what age such information should first be made available. We understand that children are not able to give true consent to sexual encounters. They do not know enough to be able to protect themselves.

Of course, if a culture's norms and rules are in extreme flux, it is possible for such boundaries to be confused or even eliminated. In times of rapid change, such as during a natural disaster or war, children are among the most vulnerable and the most common victims.

Speaking to adolescents, I have often used this imagery of the inner temple to help them understand the Church's teaching regarding sexual intimacy. There is a "narthex" of the soul, our "outer courtyard." This most public part of our lives represents the face we show to the world. It is a place of casual encounters, some of which bring joy, some of which we quickly reject. A few of the people we encounter in this way may be invited into friendship, into the "inner courtyard" or "nave" of the soul. That invitation is extended to those who can be trusted to value us, to respect the honor they have been given, and to acknowledge that they are guests here.

We also have a "holy place" that is our most intimate and delicate place. Into some portion of that place, we invite the most intimate of all human relationships—a spouse. The Church surrounds that relationship with rules and norms, not out of a fascination with a legalistic morality; instead, it is the deepest care of the soul that the Church seeks to guard. If this place is violated, particularly on a regular basis—as it is violated by sexual contact outside marriage—it begins to lose its ability to function. The result is a loss of the true self, an alienation from who we truly are, and an inability to find God.

In plain terms, if the most intimate part of the soul is turned into the most public part of the soul, the mystery is trampled underfoot. We become lost. The darkness that results manifests itself in myriad ways, none of them healthy or life-giving.

Christ taught in the Gospels that the "lamp of the body is

the eye" (Matt. 6:22). The eyes are the most prominent feature of the face. It is the face that most dramatically registers our emotions. When we experience shame, for example, blood rushes to our face (we blush) and we instinctively hide our eyes, looking down or even turning the face away. We speak of being "shamefaced" or of "losing face." Turning away is a protective reaction, one that suggests an intrusion has taken place: something or someone has crossed a boundary and sought to enter where they do not belong.

It is significant that Christ went on to warn us, "If therefore your eye is good, your whole body will be full of light. But if your eye is bad, your whole body will be full of darkness. If therefore the light that is in you is darkness, how great *is* that darkness!" (Matt. 6:22–23).

Having due regard to the boundaries of the soul is essential to our well-being. This is especially true for the young, who are truly the most vulnerable among us.

The Soul as Mirror

IN A SOMEWHAT DIFFERENT THOUGH related approach, St. Gregory of Nyssa describes the soul as a mirror. Some see in this a reference to the Platonic philosophical tradition, yet it echoes quite well a thought from the Book of Proverbs: "As in water face reflects face, / So a man's heart reveals the man" (27:19).

For Gregory, the soul reflects the image of Christ. It does this ever more clearly as we draw nearer to Him and as we remove everything that obscures that image. Catholic scholar Hans Urs von Balthasar describes Gregory's understanding:

The journey towards salvation is marked by a successive elimination of all that we "have," in order to reach what we "are." The safest path and surest refuge is not to be deluded and fail to recognize ourselves—who we truly are. We should not believe that we are seeing our Selves when we are only seeing something that surrounds us— our body, our senses, the idea that others have of us. *For anything unstable is not us.*

The soul is purified in this way, as she lays aside garment after garment. So, the ideal [salvation] will appear as that supreme instant wherein the soul, having laid aside all of her "corporeal" veils, presents herself naked and pure in spirit to the vision of God in a divine vigil.[7]

Shame and the disguises it generates within us are the primary sources of our "corporeal veils." The true self, in addition to being the gift of God—His image within us—is also a dynamic movement toward God, whose fulfillment and beauty are "being revealed." We can describe this process as eschatological. Who I am has not yet been revealed (1 John 3:2), but is "hidden with Christ in God" (Col. 3:3).

As we confront shame-related issues in our lives, this understanding will be essential. Shame sends a message that "who I am" is a problem. How deeply we experience this sense of wrongness depends on the level and nature of our shame. However, it is important, as we will see in subsequent chapters, that

---

7 Hans Urs Von Balthasar, *Presence and Thought: An Essay on the Religious Philosophy of St. Gregory of Nyssa* (San Francisco: Ignatius Press, 1995). Kindle loc. 1469 ff. Emphasis added.

we begin to understand that we ourselves are not defined by our shame; much less are we the various identities that we create in order to hide from shame.

"Anything unstable is not us." Saint Gregory's intuition is vital in the process of our healing. There is a "me" beneath the encrusted and obscured versions of the self that are generated by the dynamic of shame in our lives (as well as by other factors). It tells us that as we do the difficult work of healing, unlearning, discovery, and such (the content of repentance in the spiritual life), there is a goal that awaits us. We journey toward the true self, the image of God, the place of His true reflection, and in that place we discover that who we are stands before Him without shame or fear. This is the place of our salvation.

CHAPTER TWO

This Is Your Body on Shame

"My face was burning. My eyes were fixed on the floor. I couldn't look anyone in the face."

"I wanted to run away and hide. I felt that everyone was staring at me."

"I could have fallen through the floor."

"My hands were sweaty, and I couldn't swallow. I could feel my heart pounding. I thought I was going to be sick."

"My mind was racing. I couldn't think of what to say and almost everything I could imagine would have been inappropriate."

"I felt like I had been slapped. I was angry and sad at the same time, if that is possible. I've never been so humiliated in my life."

THESE ARE THE VOICES OF SHAME. They are common enough that all of us could have said them at one time or another. Often, they are moments that are burned into our memories and come back to haunt us. The emotions are obvious, but with them profoundly physical sensations are also taking place. These can be identified and described in clinical terms. That which we call a "feeling" is also a reaction of our bodies. Shame is among the most uncomfortable of all experiences. This is not an accident: it is supposed to feel that way.

A major question for me when I began thinking about shame was that of its origins. Where did it come from? Was it a byproduct of sin in our lives? Did it come about as a result of the Fall? My theological instincts told me that sin is death. It is not emotion or hunger or anger or fear. All the reactions of our bodies, their desires, even the things that we describe as the "passions" are never inherently evil. When they work for our destruction, or work in a manner we might designate as "sinful," they are always functioning in a distorted manner. Nothing that God created is evil. Evil is always only a distortion of the good, a parasite. As such, I reasoned, shame must have a purpose and a good side. What is it and where does it come from?

It is easy to describe hunger. When our stomachs are empty, they begin to send signals of discomfort. The discomfort tells us to eat. Unfortunately, it doesn't tell us what to eat or exactly how much. Nevertheless, to have no physical signals that told us to eat would be dangerous and destructive. Christ, we are told, fasted for forty days, and "He was hungry" (Matt. 4:2). In the same manner, shame has a physical basis and a purpose that is useful and not destructive. It is the *abuse* of shame that makes us despise and fear it.

One of the early researchers on the physical origins of shame was Silvan Tomkins. He began by noticing the reactions of infants and toddlers to certain stimuli. What he saw were not culture-driven responses, but the hardwired or instinctive reactions of very young children to their environment. These are the same for children in Africa, China, or America. Our encultur-ated reactions come later in life. It was deeply interesting to me that the hardwired responses he identified were all manifested in the *facial* expressions of a child. He described nine so-called "affects" using this observation.[8] They are distress-anguish, interest-excitement, enjoyment-joy, surprise-startle, anger-rage, fear-terror, shame-humiliation, disgust, and dissmell.

Distress-anguish is the signal that all is not well. Everyone is familiar with a baby's crying and the face that accompanies it. *Interest-excitement* is the state of being drawn toward mastery of something. It is a positive feeling that signals early development of thought and concentration. It is significant that we find it pleasurable: we *like* to learn. *Enjoyment-joy* is shown with a smile, our lips widening up and out. Tomkins found that it is triggered by a decreasing stimulus, such as a reduction in hunger or loneliness, or the relief of pain. It is of note that this affect (our showing forth of these experiences) is contagious. The child smiles and the caregiver smiles in return. Our social life begins in our very early days and months.

Surprise-startle has our eyebrows up, eyes wide, with a blink

---

8 There are any number of ways to describe the body's experience of shame. I have relied on Gershen Kaufman's explication and use of Tomkins's affect theory. See his *The Psychology of Shame: Theory and Treatment of Shame-Based Syndromes* (New York: Springer Publishing, 1989), 11–17. I find Tomkins's description quite useful, both in its simplicity and in its emphasis on the facial expressions associated with the affects. The recent work *The Body Keeps the Score* by Bessel A. van der Kolk (Penguin, 2015) focuses on how the brain processes these various experiences. Unfortunately, the brain is not immediately observable.

response. Playing peekaboo with a child is a simple way of stimulating this response. The game is fun and triggers our enjoyment as well. Laughter ensues. *Anger-rage* carries the demand to "fix it." The face becomes reddened and swollen, with muscle tension and screaming as the affect's obvious signs. *Fear-terror* comes early in life as well. It displays itself with our eyes wide open, lower eyelids tensed, eyebrows raised and drawn together. The face is pale, cold, and sweaty; hair stands on end, especially on the back of the neck. Fear is designed for emergency life-and-death situations, and it brings about an intense biological response to produce the energy needed for survival.

Shame-humiliation (which we'll examine in more detail) is brought about by the complete or partial interruption of excitement or joy. Tomkins says that the facial display is less about signaling and more about *hiding*. The eyes look down and away, the neck muscles give way and the head falls. Frequently, the face is reddened as blood runs to it. Tomkins describes the purpose of shame as a negative experience that draws our attention to whatever might have caused the positive affect (excitement or joy) to be impeded. It provides essential social information.

Disgust is an auxiliary of our hunger drive and is an impulse to spit out or expel a noxious item that has been ingested. It functions as an affect, Tomkins observed, in that there are many things that we figuratively ingest, such as people, thoughts, sights, noises. When we describe something as "disgusting" we can be quite literal in our meaning.

Similar to this is the affect of *dissmell*. It is also an auxiliary of the hunger drive but is the impulse to pull away from or push away a noxious item that shouldn't be ingested (such as dead animals, fresh feces, or sour milk). Tomkins created the word "dissmell" (analogous to "disgust," *gust* being the Latin root meaning "taste") to describe this biological response of repulsion. Its face appears with the head pulled back, the upper lip raised, the nose wrinkled, and inner ends of the eyebrows drawn downward.

It is easy to see that life in our world would be impossible (or dangerous) without these expressions of our engagement with the world around us. I have the frequent experience of reading faces as a public speaker. I would have added boredom and sleepiness to Tomkins's nine affects!

As noted, shame is not a thing in and of itself but represents a signal that something (enjoyment) has been interrupted. This need not be some intense pleasure. It may be nothing more than the enjoyment of things proceeding in the manner expected. It should also be noted that these nine affects are not independent of one another but may occur simultaneously. However, seeing shame as an interruption points to one of its primary healthy purposes. It signals *boundaries* for us.

Boundaries are distinctions we make between places we are permitted or desire to go, versus places where we are not permitted. Those places can be physical, emotional, psychological, or otherwise. In a physical setting, a boundary may be as plain as a sign that says "Authorized Personnel Only." Emotional and psychological boundaries, as well as those involved in certain social settings, are much harder to read. For example, we can be in a conversation with someone and offer a change of subject. We notice that the other person's face has changed, registering their discomfort or anger. This tells us we have crossed a boundary. It is quite possible that it is a crossing for which we had no permission. Our subsequent awkwardness will likely be experienced as shame or embarrassment (a mild form of shame). Most likely, the conversation will come to a halt, with apologies offered or new boundaries set.

In the life of a child, boundaries can be seen in simple changes of experience. For example, the experience of exposure can change a social setting, serving as a boundary that separates the safe from the unsafe. I have frequently encountered mothers with toddlers in their arms. Leaning in and addressing the baby (as in the case of giving communion), it is not unusual to be met with a look of discomfort, the child burying her face in her mother's arms. The encounter has made the child feel exposed and vulnerable. Her instinctive reaction is an early presentation of shame. It is not shame in our adult sense of the experience, but it is triggered in the same manner.

Unwanted exposure is one of many such triggers. Another is disappointed expectation. Unrequited love and exclusion are primary triggers as well, particularly as we begin to move out of the home and into social settings.[9] The phenomenon of boundaries is quite complicated, particularly in a social context, and can vary greatly depending on cultures. Most cultures have ways of communicating shame as a means of inculcating boundaries. We learn that certain subjects are not to be discussed in certain settings, or that certain behaviors are not tolerated in various places. The experience of such enculturated

---

9   Joseph Burgo's *Shame* (New York: St. Martin's Press, 2018) gives a very readable account of the most common triggers of shame with a helpful discussion of each.

shame may be short in duration and relatively painless. It can also be profound and devastating.

Unbounded and Toxic Shame

SHAME HAS A WAY OF breaking through our own internal boundaries. Because it triggers feelings of exposure or exclusion, shame can be deeply wounding. The emotions that shaming events trigger (which are themselves labeled "shame") are often associated with the question, "Who am I?" This question points towards the *dissociative* character of shame: it can make us feel alien even to ourselves, as though we were standing outside ourselves and watching (and not liking what we see).

Questions of identity abound, particularly in the lives of adolescents and teens. This is perfectly natural in that who a person is can be in a profound state of flux at such an age. We do not come with a fixed, static personality that we then present to the world. Instead, we constantly receive signals about ourselves from those around us, from the deep affirmation of a mother's love to the taunting of a bully in the hallway at middle school.

My first encounter with bullying was in second grade. At recess early in the year, another boy began to taunt me with laughter and cries of "baby shoes!" I wore special corrective shoes for a foot problem. The shoes looked, admittedly, like the little high-tops commonly worn by babies. I had not noticed the resemblance until that moment. It was a moment of separation, a distancing from myself. I wanted not to be the boy with those shoes. This episode became an occasion of separation from my mother as I began to insist that I needed to wear something more acceptable. As minor as the matter was in hindsight, it became part of a larger pattern of toxic shaming. I was smaller than most of the boys in my class and not competitive athletically. "Baby shoes" was only one of many nicknames that came my way.

I did a poor job of integrating myself into that environment. The various adaptations we take on in response to toxic shaming are never truly successful. The bullied child can become a bully, or a perfectionist, or, worse still (for me), a sycophant, easily agreeing with his bullies, wanting approval and acceptance.

Such strategies are common. They represent efforts to construct an identity that is safe and protected, in which we are able to hide from the shame that has driven us into such positions. Rather than nurturing the soul, these efforts become distractions and deviations from the path to wholeness. That same lack of integration creates a loneliness and an abiding alienation as we wait for signals to reassure us that we are loved and accepted, or at least safe from the winds of toxic shaming.

The pain of toxic shame can come from many places: the immediate family, close friends, authority figures, and others. We can become so deeply alienated from ourselves that we become our own bullies, taking up the taunts as our own and torturing ourselves with disapproval and disdain. The personality of toxic shame is never safe—we become our own worst enemies.

Trauma is another source of such toxic experiences. Those who have been victims of violence, either physical or emotional, can take up the positions of their tormenters, blaming themselves for what took place, internalizing the pain in such a manner that lack of safety becomes the default position of the inner life.

One way to think of toxic shame is to see it as a severe loss of boundaries. Adults recovering from such shame often need to undertake the difficult task of creating boundaries. They need to find the self that lies beneath the various shame-induced strategies and begin to affirm and nurture it in the inherent dignity given to each of us by God. At the same time, they need to establish inner and outer rules that govern what and who will be allowed to enter into relationship or conversation with them. Often, establishing boundaries involves the painful work of dismantling the habits of a lifetime. It cannot be done alone—we need assistance.

One difficulty with boundaries is that healthy shame, the primary signaling ability that is part of us from birth, is itself the *normative* means of signaling boundaries within ourselves. When, for example, we enter a room of strangers, we read behaviors, how people are dressed, how they speak. If any of these things present problems for us, we will likely experience discomfort of some sort. We might say we are "embarrassed" or "feel awkward." What we are in fact experiencing is healthy shame, a natural signal that draws our attention to potential issues. Healthy shame is a necessary part of a social existence. It is an emotional signal that indicates various boundaries, some of which may be so subtle that we have no words for them.

With toxic shame, the experience that something is wrong has moved beyond a mere signal and become embedded in the personality itself. In various ways, toxic shame takes over the personality and begins to dictate our identity. We may find ourselves acting out in a social setting, playing a role that seeks to protect the self even from normal, healthy shame. In a personality encumbered by toxic shame, even healthy shame can *feel* toxic. So-called narcissistic personalities are said by some to be unable to tolerate any shame, making them unable to bear the presence of any boundary. They refuse to accept responsibility for their own actions (and any shame that might accompany a misdeed) while violating the boundaries of others, seeking to deflect all shame from themselves.

The difficult dance between healthy shame and a healthy personality is born of the fact that these two need one another. I cannot be who I truly am without accepting the legitimacy of who I am not. If, as is often the case for those laboring under the burden of unresolved toxic shame, my inner life is a constant chorus of shame, singing my own litany of failures and disappointments, then I will be deaf to the legitimate song of another's excellence. Every such song will likely be heard only as another condemnation, a reminder of what I am not but imagine I should be.

There is a dynamic quality in all of this. Popular psychology speaks of "self-esteem," a proper human need in a healthy life. Critics suggest that too much attention to self-esteem creates weak personalities that are unable to withstand criticism and nurtures an unrealistic estimation of one's own excellence. The false choice of an either-or ignores the importance of both a deeply valued core and appropriate boundaries—which means the acceptance of healthy shame.

For Christian believers, *healthy* shame plays an essential role. It has a primary place in the encounter with God. I recall an old-timer from Alcoholics Anonymous saying, "The only thing you need to know about God is that you're not Him." The German theologian Rudolf Otto, in his seminal work *The Idea of the Holy* (1917), suggested that the encounter with God is an apprehension of the "Wholly Other" (*Ganz Anders*). He carefully described the human feeling of *awe* that comes with such encounters. Psychologist John Bradshaw wrote that healthy shame is utterly essential in the experience of awe—indeed, such awe is itself a species of healthy shame.[10]

We see these encounters, along with the boundaries that are revealed in them, in Scripture. Moses is drawn by the sight of a burning bush but is warned to stop and remove his shoes before drawing close. Isaiah has a vision of God on His throne of glory, surrounded by the seraphim. His own reaction is to say, "Woe is me, for . . . I am a man of unclean lips, / And I dwell in the midst of a people of unclean lips" (Is. 6:5). He perceives God, but in so doing also perceives himself. His cry regarding his uncleanness is not the voice of toxic shame. Rather, it is a healthy response to the Holy, that which is utterly clean. The Holy serves as a mirror, and in it, Isaiah is able to see himself as he truly is. The Holy, however, does not reveal Himself in order to condemn Isaiah. Instead, an angel brings a coal of fire from the throne and touches it to the prophet's lips, making him clean and whole. His shame is addressed, and he becomes the messenger of God.

This encounter is a small model of shame and the knowledge of God. God is not part of the chorus of condemning voices. It is worth noting that the cry of Isaiah comes from within himself—it is not the voice of God condemning him. I often have recourse to this understanding when helping people rightly see

---

10 John Bradshaw, *Healing the Shame that Binds You* (Health Communications, Inc., 2005), 18.

and understand the traditional prayers we find in our prayer-books. These prayers are ancient poetry, written by lovers of God who have encountered the Holy, seen their own broken-ness, and written from the fullness that comes from the heal-ing brought about within them. The language of those prayers is often misheard and interpreted as though it were the voice of the Church shaming its members. It is nothing of the sort.

Healthy Shame and Humility

REPEATEDLY IN THE TRADITION, THE experience of healthy shame is described under the heading of "humility." Humil-ity is not the degradation of the self, much less some version of self-shaming. Rather, it is the acceptance of the boundaries around us that are real and true. To see the excellence in oth-ers or the wonder of the creation itself does not require that I despise myself or dismiss any sense of self-worth. It is, to a great extent, the opposite. Those who despise themselves and dismiss their self-worth are likely reacting to toxic shame and thereby rendering themselves incapable of accurately seeing or appreci-ating what is around them. Toxic shame destroys boundaries, making the world and everything around us to be "about us." The excellence of the other becomes an occasion for despising myself. It is a path toward a form of narcissism and the loneli-ness of a shame-generated alienation.

Healthy shame, even when voiced in the poetry of wonder and self-abasement, recognizes the otherness of what is outside the self. If the language of humility seems to diminish the self, it does so only in order to *enlarge* the self in the proper unity with the world that is the truth of personhood.

The most fundamental relationship in our human existence is that of *communion*. We are not born as independent creatures but as infants, dependent on adults for food and every form of care. Among the most primary of those needs is the bond of love, expressed in communion. It is of note that this physical and emotional bond is also expressed in the face. As a child nurses, he or she experiences facial bonding with a mother or caregiver. That facial interaction is just as necessary as the food the child receives.

Research famously known as the "still face experiment" illustrates this bond. In 1975, Edward Tronick and his associates created an experiment

> in which an infant, after three minutes of "interaction" with a non-responsive expressionless mother, "rapidly sobers and grows wary. He makes repeated attempts to get the interaction into its usual reciprocal pattern. When these attempts fail, the infant withdraws [and] orients his face and body away from his mother with a withdrawn, hopeless facial expression." It remains one of the most replicated findings in developmental psychology.[11]

The heart sinks at the words "withdrawn, hopeless facial expression." The rupture in communion is the deepest wound of all and lies beneath every experience of shame. Tragic reports from Eastern Europe after the fall of Communism revealed state orphanages in which children had been deeply neglected, particularly in terms of holding and human interaction. These

---

11 "The Research: The Still Face Experiment," *The Gottman Institute*, https://www.gottman.com/blog/research-still-face-experiment/.

institutions housed children who were suffering and dying from what was termed "failure to thrive." It was not food they lacked; it was *communion*—particularly that expressed in skin-to-skin contact and facial bonding.

Shame disrupts the most fundamental needs in our lives and, in its most extreme forms, becomes a source of death. Perhaps more frightening is the fact that those bound in toxic shame endure a living death in the form of alienation and lack of communion—even with themselves.

These are facts that point toward the centrality of shame as a theological and pastoral concern. They go to the very heart of our existence and the nature of our salvation. What we label as the Fall is nothing other than the rupture of communion between God and human beings. It is no accident that the Genesis account mentions shame as our first emotion in that rupture. How could it have been otherwise? Shame is what broken communion feels like.

We will be looking at the theology of broken communion and its healing, particularly within the Orthodox Tradition. Other than death itself, nothing more aptly describes our brokenness than the phenomenon of shame. We will see that Isaiah, who saw God on His throne, also foretold the coming of a Messiah, the "Suffering Servant," who would not "hide [His] face from shame and spitting" (50:6). The reality of shame is a proper lens for understanding our condition as well as the work of God in our world that we describe as salvation. It provides a guide for pastoral care as well as theology. It allows us to discover the wonder of God within ourselves as, beholding the face of Christ, we grow from glory to glory.

CHAPTER THREE

An Atonement of Shame

CONSIDER THE CASE of a *sick* man versus a *guilty* man. A sick man elicits sympathy. We are concerned about how the sickness affects his body and his mind. We are concerned about the outcome of the sickness and its effects on those around him. We care for him. We raise money for his family. We praise the doctors and nurses who minister to him, seeing them as heroes. We see his sickness as an enemy, something to be vanquished and defeated. If his sickness kills him, we mourn, and we work hard to keep this scenario from being repeated in others. We comfort those who grieve his passing.

The guilty man is another thing altogether. The guilty man has a legal problem. His actions are a violation of the law. The law presumes that the man could have done otherwise and has freely chosen to transgress. Thus, the law will punish him, assuming that painful consequences will persuade him to make better choices. We think of his lawbreaking as something that needs to be paid for. If he is imprisoned, we say that he is paying his debt to society. The guilty man needs to pay for what he has done.

These two scenarios could be understood as two ways of seeing the same person. Both kinds of person have something wrong with them. The sick man has a disease that is destroying his body and possibly his mind. The guilty man has broken rules. The sick man has a problem within himself. The guilty man has a problem outside himself. The sick man needs to be cured. Nothing else will save him. The guilty man would be perfectly fine if he had not offended against the law. In himself he is fine.

These two scenarios can be a shorthand for understanding the problem of sin. If the Christian Faith is the story of a good God who loves humanity to such an extent that He comes in person to save us, then we are right to ask, "Save us from what?" St. Paul said (in what is undoubtedly a quote from a very primitive, early creed), "Christ died for our sins according to the Scriptures" (1 Cor. 15:3). But what is the story of sin? Is our problem like that of the sick man or the guilty man? The answer to that question has a way of determining the entire thrust of Christian understanding. It also has much to tell us about the place of shame within that story.

The Sin of the Guilty Man

I WAS RAISED IN THE world of the guilty man. In the land of the free and the home of the brave, what mattered most was the choices you made. The culture of Southern Protestantism was not dominated by strong, classical ideas. The intellectual rigor of Calvinism had waned sometime in the previous century. What took its place were various offshoots of nineteenth-century revival-based Christianity. Like the country itself, such

Christianity and its adherents were largely "self-made." We are what we *choose* to be. The revival-style preaching was always geared toward "making a decision for Christ."

In my little Sunday school class, I can recall being urged to sign the pledge. I must have been around eight or nine when this choice was set before me. The pledge was a promise to touch neither alcohol nor tobacco before the age of twenty-one. The assumption, I think, was that if you waited that long you would likely never acquire such bad habits. Of course, it was also true that in the early sixties, almost all adults smoked. Smoking was everywhere. Drinking was also common, though often done on the sly in that culture. The failure of the pledge, I suspect, was that it was asking me not to be like my father or any of the other men I knew. That was a losing proposition.

The emphasis on choice and free will is a natural component of a culture driven by consumerism. The notion that our choices and decisions are at the very center of our life, the actions that give us purpose and meaning, is simply one of the unexamined ideas that permeate the world around us. It has strong implications, however, when we begin to think about what is wrong with us.

One feature of our assumptions about free will is the place of punishment in our culture. To my knowledge, every kid on my street (and there were many of them in my baby-boom world) was subject to vigorous physical punishment. Some parents preferred "switches" (small branches torn from shrubs), others used various household tools (hairbrushes, spatulas, etc.), while the most robust employed a belt. My parents were very robust. Interestingly, the punishment was not always immediate. It was not used to stop an action. Instead, it could come much later in the day. The most terrible phrase I could hear was "Wait till your father gets home." How awful it must have been to come home from a day of hard labor only to be told that you needed to whip a child!

The necessity of punishment in our culture is an important context in which to think about the guilty man. Our preachers told us that our wrongdoing incurred a debt. That debt required punishment. In my teen years, when the first theological explanations were given to us, we were told that God is a "just God," and that His justice required that we be punished for what we had done wrong. Much of that made sense in terms of the way parental punishment was meted out. The long wait through a day for a promised punishment to be delivered by my father was not subject to alteration. Whatever the offense had been, it *required* a whipping. No amount of begging or promising could change what was coming. Repentance was useless. Indeed, the threat of guaranteed punishment was assumed to be the only guarantor of repentance. People do not want to be punished. Punishment is a means of managing human misbehavior. You have free will, but it can be controlled if it is motivated by the choice to avoid pain.

An aspect of this free will-oriented society was (and is) its attention to outward conformity and its inattention to what might be taking place within a person. The formula of free will, driven by incentives (pain and pleasure), offered a simple description of the world. Do good, and you will be rewarded. Do bad, and you will be punished. This creates a moralistic culture. That moralism has enjoyed a place of great honor in

FACE TO FACE

American history, often forming the basis for various political movements.[12]

In theological terms, this same pattern can be discerned particularly in various prominent strains of thought that came to be dominant in Western Christianity. Its most classical treatment is termed *penal substitutionary atonement*. This holds that human wrongdoing (sin) incurs a debt against the justice of God. Thus, we are deserving of punishment. Of course, this is deeply tied to various teachings regarding eternal punishment in hell. In the sin-as-legal-guilt world, it is sometimes said that, since the justice of God is infinite, so a sin against it is infinite and therefore deserving of infinite punishment. Eternal punishment in hell thus becomes a one-size-fits-all justice for guilty humanity.

Such offenses against a sense of justice, in my experience, are the sort of stuff that creates a breeding ground for atheism. When I was thirteen years old, I committed my first act of blasphemy. It occurred to me during a theological conversation with a friend (if you can call it that) in which the legal approach to sin and punishment seemed to represent a "God problem." In other words, the offense was a problem for God (or His justice). I recall saying that "if God would just relax, we could all go to heaven." I added to that my blasphemy, "If God is sending anyone to hell, then I don't want to go to heaven." This came at the beginning of a two-year period of nonattendance at church

---

12 American politics, particularly when married to various social causes, has almost always taken strong moral positions. This is true of both left and right, both Christian and nonreligious. It is probably impossible to tell the story of America without reference to its many religious movements—it is a nation whose self-understanding is essentially religious in nature. See Eugene McCarraher, *The Enchantments of Mammon: How Capitalism Became the Religion of Modernity* (Cambridge, MA: Harvard University Press, 2019).

while knocking about in various versions of unbelief. My sympathy for anyone who has run afoul of this sort of thinking and ended up as an unbeliever is quite strong. It's for this reason that I often say to atheists, "Tell me about the God you don't believe in. I probably don't believe in that one either."

Understanding sin in legal terms, as a violation of God's justice with an accompanying sin-debt, leaves unattended the interior life of human beings. Sin is seen as something purely exterior to our existence, a violation of rules created by our wrong decisions and choices. This is a profoundly inadequate account of our life and the mystery of who we are. As important as choices and decisions might be, they come at the end of a long chain of experience that consists of everything from genetics to cultural inheritance to incalculable factors that figure as part of our identity. This approach is also inadequate as a treatment of sin as presented in the Scriptures. It is worth remembering that St. Paul declares that Christ died for our sins "in accordance with the Scriptures." He himself provides an interesting look at sin within the human life.

What Is Sin?

IN ROMANS 7, PAUL PUTS forward an extremely interiorized view of sin:

> I do not understand my own actions. For I do not do what I want, but I do the very thing I hate. . . . So then it is no longer I that do it, but sin which dwells within me. For I know that nothing good dwells within me, that is, in my flesh. I can will what is right, but I cannot do it. For I do

not do the good I want, but the evil I do not want is what I do. Now if I do what I do not want, it is no longer I that do it, but sin which dwells within me. (vv. 15–20, RSV)

St. Paul is echoing observations that had become part of Jewish thought long before his time. Rabbinical scholars postulated that there were two impulses in human beings—an impulse for good and an impulse for evil. These were discussed in a variety of ways. Here, St. Paul is naming this impulse toward evil "sin which dwells in me." In this language, a distinction is drawn between the self ("I do not do what I want") and the impulse (sin) that pushes it toward evil. We need to see that, however difficult it may be to describe or understand, this impulse toward evil is somehow *alien* to us. It even acts *contrary to what we want*.

This is the biblical story of sin. In the Genesis account of the first sin, the man and woman are not described as primarily driven by their choices. The first sin comes from an outside suggestion (the serpent). In the New Testament, St. Paul describes Eve as having been "deceived" rather than as making a well-informed but wrong decision (2 Cor. 11:3).

The Tradition of the Eastern Church largely avoided the concept of the guilty man that came to dominate the Christian West. Instead, sin was largely understood in terms of disease, a force that comes from outside us and yet is within us, corrupting us like a cancer.

In the canons of the Sixth Ecumenical Council, an interesting take on sin is offered as part of the definitive teaching of the Church. Canon 102 reads:

It behooves those who have received from God the power to loose and bind, to consider the quality of the sin and the readiness of the sinner for conversion, and to apply medicine suitable for the disease, lest if he is injudicious in each of these respects he should fail in regard to the healing of the sick man. For the disease of sin is not simple, but various and multiform, and it germinates many mischievous offshoots, from which much evil is diffused, and it proceeds further until it is checked by the power of the physician. Wherefore he who professes the science of spiritual medicine ought first of all to consider the disposition of him who has sinned, and to see whether he tends to health or (on the contrary) provokes to himself disease by his own behavior, and to look how he can care for his manner of life during the interval.

This canon repeats what had become a commonplace in the Eastern Church. Sin is a "disease," and the ministry of the Church is the "science of spiritual medicine." In the second century, St. Ignatius of Antioch described the Eucharist as the "medicine of immortality." Centuries of monastic discipline in the deserts of Egypt and Palestine were not oriented toward battles against a legal problem, an effort to pay a legal debt. Rather, they were centuries of research in the hard experience of the daily battle against sin—"various and multiform." In guarding the heart and courageously entering the secret recesses of our inner experience, the monks found a sort of psychology (literally, "the science of the soul") in which they learned about the nature of the disease as well as the science of its cure.

An Atonement of Shame

DIFFERENT FUNDAMENTAL UNDERSTANDINGS OF THE nature of sin give rise to the various ways Christians speak about Christ's death on the Cross. For those who see sin in terms of a legal debt against the justice of God, Christ's death will be described as a payment, His accepting of a punishment that He Himself did not deserve but that is owed by us. Quite often, the stories and art that surround this account are marked by a focus on pain and suffering. What is taking place on the Cross is an infinite payment for an infinite debt. Therefore, it cannot possibly be exaggerated in terms of its terrible suffering. Every wrong thing ever done by any human being is being paid for by this one single death. Interestingly, in this view, the Resurrection of Christ seems to be something of an afterthought, merely an indication that the payment has been accepted and that all is now well.

In the Eastern Church, the language of the atonement story is quite different. It does not focus so much on pain as on shame. It also tends to see Christ as one who fights on our behalf, both within us and outside us. This takes us into a narrative that will seem familiar in some ways and strange in others. It is, however, the oldest narrative in the Christian Tradition.

From within that Tradition we have this statement (quoted earlier):

> The heart itself is but a small vessel, yet there also are dragons and there are lions; there are poisonous beasts and all the treasures of evil ... there is also God, also the angels, the life and the kingdom, the light and the Apostles, the

treasures of grace—there are all things. (Macarian Homilies H.43.7)

This statement reveals the imagery and understanding that are often at work in Orthodox thought. It speaks of outer things: God, angels, the Kingdom, light, the apostles, heavenly cities. But it comfortably places all of them within the confines of the heart, "but a small vessel." In a similar manner, St. Maximus the Confessor describes human beings as a "microcosm," that is, as the universe (*cosmos*) made small (*micro*). This indicates that though we may speak of things outside ourselves (heaven, hell, sin, death, the Kingdom, and so forth), they are also within us. We are not strangers to such things—they are the stuff of which we are made. The narrative of Christ, His Cross, and His death and Resurrection is also the narrative of our inner life. What He is doing *for* us, He also does *within* us.

In the hymns and services of Holy Week and Pascha we hear the loudest refrains of this primitive narrative. The New Testament gathers some of these themes within itself. In Isaiah, we hear the foretelling of a coming Messiah who will deliver His people.

I gave My back to those who struck *Me*,
And My cheeks to those who plucked out the beard;
I did not hide My face from shame and spitting.
(Is. 50:6)

This theme of humiliation and mocking reverberates throughout the Orthodox texts for the feasts. Saint Paul recalls this as well:

Let this mind be in you which was also in Christ Jesus, who, being in the form of God, did not consider it robbery to be equal with God, but made Himself of no reputation, taking the form of a bondservant, *and* coming in the likeness of men. And being found in appearance as a man, He humbled Himself and became obedient to *the point of* death, even the death of the cross. Therefore, God also has highly exalted Him and given Him the name which is above every name, that at the name of Jesus every knee should bow, of those in heaven, and of those on earth, and of those under the earth, and *that* every tongue should confess that Jesus Christ is Lord, to the glory of God the Father. (Phil. 2:5–11)

Scholars believe this passage in St. Paul's letter is quoting an early Christian hymn, which would demonstrate that this theme had already become embedded in the liturgical life of the early Church. The drama of salvation is described in this divine reversal: God has come among us in Christ, emptying Himself of His glory. Instead of glory, He enters into shame—even the shameful death of the Cross. And entering into that shameful death, He destroys death and ascends in glory. He conquers death by death. He overcomes shame by shame.

We are unaccustomed in our culture to thinking of sin and shame as sharing a connection. We have been formed and shaped in the world of guilt and punishment. If we experience shame, we suppose, it is because other people are seeking to shame us. Thus we are likely to imagine that the shame in our lives is external, the result of social ills. If we fix society, our shame will disappear. This is not a surprising approach, given that our habits have long been directed toward sin as an external problem. But other people, regardless of our situation, are not our problem. The French philosopher Jean-Paul Sartre said, "Hell is other people." He must not have spent much time alone.

Sin is much better understood as disease, fatal in its consequences. Sin, in a form of shorthand, can be described as "death at work within us." At its most fundamental level, sin is the rupture of communion. We were created for a life of communion with God. In our sin, we have severed that communion and become strangers to God. Indeed, we have become strangers not only to God but to creation, to other people, even to ourselves. In an interesting side note, the secular shame researcher Gershen Kaufman describes shame as "broken communion."[13] Shame itself is not sin (or even sinful). Rather, it is an emotional signal that accompanies severed communion. It is, therefore, one of the things that sin feels like.

In the Church's icon of the Resurrection, Christ is depicted as having descended into hell. He takes Adam and Eve by the hand in order to lead them out. An ancient homily on Christ's encounter with Adam in Hades, believed to have been written by Epiphanius of Salamis, says:

At the sight of him Adam, the first man he had created, struck his breast in terror and cried out to everyone, "My Lord be with you all." Christ answered him: "And with your spirit." He took him by the hand and raised him up, saying:

---

13 Kaufman, *Psychology of Shame*, 32–33.

"Awake, O sleeper, and rise from the dead, and Christ will give you light.

"I am your God, who for your sake have become your son. Out of love for you and your descendants I now by my own authority command all who are held in bondage to come forth, all who are in darkness to be enlightened, all who are sleeping to arise. I order you, O sleeper, to awake. I did not create you to be held a prisoner in Hell. Rise from the dead, for I am the life of the dead. Rise up, work of my hands, you who were created in my image. Rise, let us leave this place, for you are in Me and I in you; together we form one person and cannot be separated. . . .

"See on My Face the spittle I received in order to restore to you the life I once breathed into you. See there the marks of the blows I received in order to refashion your warped nature in my image. On My back see the marks of the scourging I endured to remove the burden of sin that weighs upon your back. See My hands, nailed firmly to a tree, for you who once wickedly stretched out your hand to a tree. . . .

"Rise, let us leave this place. The enemy led you out of the earthly Paradise. I will not restore you to that Paradise, but will enthrone you in heaven. I forbade you the tree that was only a symbol of life, but see, I who am life itself am now one with you. . . . The Bridal Chamber is adorned, the banquet is ready, the eternal dwelling places are prepared, the treasure houses of all good things lie open. The Kingdom of Heaven has been prepared for you from all eternity."[14]

If this scene is extended to the heart of the believer (as in the quote from the Macarian Homilies), it can be understood as a contemporary dialogue for each of us as we confront Christ in the self-made hell of our own soul. The shame we experience in our broken communion is overcome, not by a God who ignores our shame, but by a God who Himself takes that shame for His own.

My own experience of shame has been one of extreme loneliness and alienation. Shame comes to us as a blow to our ability to reason. We cannot think our way out of it. Indeed, because shame shatters even our communion with the self, it has the potential effect of creating a false self. We become uncertain of who or what is described by the term "self." Of course, shame can be anything from mild embarrassment to a deep, toxic wound. The effects of its inner estrangement have a similar range.

An Atonement of Communion

THE FACT THAT SHAME IS directly tied to the experience of communion, becoming an emotion triggered by the interruption of communion, indicates that it also has a direct connection to the sacramental life of the Church. For the sacramental life is, *par excellence*, the life of communion.

---

14 The Lord's descent into hell, Pontifical University of St. Thomas Aquinas, https://www.vatican.va/spirit/documents/spirit_20010414_omelia-sabato-santo_en.html

In the service of Holy Baptism, in one of the standard English translations, the candidates are asked, "Do you unite yourself to Christ?" They respond, "I do unite myself to Christ!" This is repeated three times. This expresses the very heart of the sacrament. In the blessing of the baptismal waters, we hear a range of descriptions of what is taking place:

> But show this water, O Master of all, to be the water of redemption, the water of sanctification, the purification of flesh and spirit, the loosing of bonds, the remission of sins, the illumination of the soul, the washing of regeneration, the renewal of the Spirit, the gift of adoption to sonship, the garment of incorruption, the fountain of life.[15]

Redemption, sanctification, purification, loosing of bonds, remission of sins, illumination, washing, renewal, adoption, garment of incorruption, fountain—all in one action!

I have often been amused to hear explanations of baptism from Christians outside Orthodoxy. Frequently, these explanations represent a diminishment of the event, an attempt to speak in careful, narrow terms. The primitive Tradition of Orthodoxy, on the other hand, seems to be reaching for every possible image to describe what is taking place. Baptism, like all the sacraments, is not a narrowing—it is an enlargement and a fullness.

Holy Baptism can be all the things described in the prayer because it is a union, a communion, with Christ.

---

15 *Baptism* (New York: Department of Religious Education, Orthodox Church in America, 1972), 51–52. I have rendered the passage in contemporary English for ease of reading.

Or do you not know that as many of us as were baptized into Christ Jesus were baptized into His death? Therefore, we were buried with Him through baptism into death, that just as Christ was raised from the dead by the glory of the Father, even so we also should walk in newness of life. (Rom. 6:3–4)

And, "For as many of you as were baptized into Christ have put on Christ" (Gal. 3:27).

This language of union is found throughout the New Testament. Saint Paul describes himself as being "crucified with Christ," adding that "it is no longer I who live, but Christ lives in me" (Gal. 2:20).

The same kind of language is used when the Scriptures speak of the Eucharist. Saint Paul calls it a "communion" (*koinonia*). "The cup of blessing which we bless, is it not the communion of the blood of Christ? The bread which we break, is it not the communion of the body of Christ?" (1 Cor. 10:16).

In John 6, we hear Christ Himself teaching about the Eucharist. The entire discourse is directed toward the mystery of union or communion with Him:

"I am the living bread which came down from heaven. If anyone eats of this bread, he will live forever; and the bread that I shall give is My flesh, which I shall give for the life of the world. . . . Most assuredly, I say to you, unless you eat the flesh of the Son of Man and drink His blood, you have no life in you. Whoever eats My flesh and drinks My blood has eternal life, and I will raise him up at the last day. For My flesh is food indeed, and My blood is drink indeed. He who eats My flesh and drinks My blood abides in Me, and I in him." (John 6:51, 53–56)

We were created to live in communion with God. His life is our life. When we read about the creation of Adam, we see that he becomes a "living soul" when God breathes into him. Without the life of God, we are dead clay. The warning regarding the Tree of the Knowledge of Good and Evil is not a threat of punishment; rather, it is a warning that eating of it will result in death. To break communion with God by ignoring His commandment is to live as though we had no need of God. It is to spit His breath back at Him and demand that we live alone. The result is death, and with the alienation of death, we enter into its companion: shame.

If the loss of communion is both the beginning and the very nature of sin, then the restoration of communion is the beginning and the very nature of salvation. It is also the nature of the divine therapy that heals our shame.

Just as the sacrament of baptism invokes a variety of images in its liturgical expression, so too the atonement, the restoration of our communion with God, is described with a variety of images. Theories such as penal substitutionary atonement that seek to reduce Christ's death on the Cross to a transactional payment, something to satisfy the abstraction of God's justice, have the effect of diminishing both the doctrine of the atonement and the Faith as a whole. The problem of sin is not outside us. It is not a legal problem created by God's unwavering demands. It is the manifestation of a human life cut off from God. Human life apart from God is, in the end, no life at all. To this, Christ says, "I have come that they may have life, and that they may have *it* more abundantly" (John 10:10).

CHAPTER FOUR

Where Fools Rush In

No one enjoys the experience of shame. It is painful and humiliating. Some, however, enter it willingly. Comedians will sometimes place themselves in shameful positions or describe others in a shameful manner. Certain forms of shame elicit laughter. I'll have more to say about that later. We find the shame of others to be entertaining if it is presented in the right way. Shame can also be therapeutic if rightly understood and endured. That is a much more difficult topic, though it has an important place in the Tradition.

In the early seventies, between high school and college, I would have been rightly described as a "Jesus freak." I was living in a commune, working in a factory (among other things), and "doing ministry" such as I found it. Such ministry mostly consisted of telling others about Jesus, conducting prayer groups, and being involved in a local house church. Among the ministries we undertook was work on a local college campus. As the fall semester began one year, I made plans to drop in on the campus and see who was there and what was going on. I recall getting dressed that morning. The thought crossed my mind that I would encounter girls. I started thinking about what I should wear.

At the same time, the conscience of a Jesus freak arose within me with a strong rebuke. The vanity and darker thoughts involved in getting dressed needed attention. So that day, I chose to dress in a manner that would make me appear ridiculous (I'll not share the details). It was an intentional act of self-shaming as a means of discipline. Of course, had I taken myself less seriously, I wouldn't have needed such a discipline, but I was young and full of myself. As it turned out, I have had cause to remember that strange occasion very well, for it was the day I first met the girl who would later become my wife. Providence has its own jokes to play.

I didn't know it at the time, but my action was exceedingly "traditional." The voluntary bearing of shame, generally called by other names, has long been a part of Christian ascesis. It is a difficult and bitter medicine, but rightly managed, it can be a profound component in the life of repentance.

Stories from the early centuries of Christianity, particularly those drawn from the lives of the desert monastics, recall both great successes and great failures in the spiritual life. Desert monasticism was a vast spiritual experiment. The words and teachings of the Scriptures were often applied with both great zeal and great creativity. The record of what worked eventually became the basis of the various rules that govern Christian monasticism to this day. This environment also constituted a furnace in which the dross was burnt away from the precious metals of men's and women's souls. Much of the wisdom that shaped canon law came out of that fiery trial. It remains a deep source of understanding for our contemporary world. Human beings, despite the changes in culture over the centuries, have remained unchanged. It is a mistake to imagine ourselves to be different, much less superior.

The following story is taken from *The Ladder of Divine Ascent*, written in the sixth century by St. John Climacus, who ended his life as the abbot of St. Catherine's Monastery on Mt. Sinai. St. John traveled, collected stories from monasteries of his time, and published them in what is now one of the greatest classics of the spiritual life. This story gives an insight into an experiment in therapeutic shame.

Terrible indeed was the judgment of a good judge and shepherd which I once saw in a monastery. For while I was there, it happened that a robber applied for admission to the monastic life. And that most excellent pastor and physician ordered him to take seven days of complete rest, just to see the kind of life in the place.

When the week had passed, the pastor called him and asked him privately: "Would you like to live with us?" And when he saw that he agreed to this with all sincerity, he then asked him what evil he had done in the world. And when he saw that he readily confessed everything, he tried him still further, and said: "I want you to tell this in the presence of all the brethren." But he really did hate his sin, and, scorning all shame, without the least hesitation he promised to do it. "And if you like," he said, "I will tell it in the middle of the city of Alexandria."

And so, the shepherd gathered all his sheep in the church, to the number of 230, and during Divine Liturgy (for it was Sunday), after the reading of the Gospel, he introduced this irreproachable convict. He was dragged by several of the brethren, who gave him moderate blows. His hands were tied behind his back, he was dressed in a hair shirt, his head was sprinkled with ashes. All were astonished at the sight. And immediately a woeful cry rang out, for no one knew what was happening.

Then, when the robber appeared at the doors of the nave, that holy superior who had such love for souls said to him in a loud voice: "Stop! You are not worthy to enter here."

Dumbfounded by the voice of the shepherd coming from the sanctuary (for he thought, as he afterwards assured us with oaths, that he had heard not a human voice, but thunder), he instantly fell on his face, trembling and shaking all over with fear. As he lay on the ground and moistened the floor with his tears, this wonderful physician, using all means for his salvation, and wishing to give to all an example of saving and effectual humility, again exhorted him, in the presence of all, to tell in detail what he had done.

And with terror he confessed one after another all his sins, which revolted every ear, not only sins of the flesh, natural and unnatural, with rational beings and with animals, but even poisoning, murder and many other kinds which it is indecent to hear or commit to writing. And when he had finished his confession, the shepherd at once allowed him to be given the habit and numbered among the brethren.

Amazed by the wisdom of that holy man, I asked him when we were alone: "Why did you make such an extraordinary show?" That true physician replied: "For two reasons: firstly, in order to deliver the penitent himself from future shame by present shame; and it really did that, Brother John. For he did not rise from the floor until he was granted remission of all his sins. And do not doubt this, for one of the brethren who was there confided to me, saying: "I saw someone terrible [an angel] holding a pen and writing-tablet, and as the prostrate man told each sin, he crossed it out with a pen." And this is likely, for it says: I said, I will confess against myself my sin to the Lord; and Thou hast forgiven the wickedness of my heart (Psalm 31:5). Secondly, because there are others in the brotherhood who have unconfessed sins, and I want to induce them to confess too, for without this no one will obtain forgiveness."[16]

Readers of this story should bear in mind the extreme measure of this man's wrongdoing. The list of crimes he reported would normally have locked him away in prison for the rest of his life or placed his neck at the end of a rope. His shame was the deep shame of a life ill-spent. He certainly could have continued in that way of life, avoiding his shame in the constant shamelessness of wanton crime. His criminality had become a false identity. I'm reminded of the humorous saying, "Yea, though I

---

16 Book 4, 11. The translation has been adapted from that of Lazarus Moore.

walk through the valley of death, I will fear no evil. For I'm the meanest guy in the valley."

This man's journey, however, was toward a wholeness that could only be found in exposing the truth of his life. We should not imagine that his forgiveness and being clothed as a monk suddenly freed him from every responsibility incurred through his crimes. His life as a monk, under the strict regime of the desert, would make the life of today's prison inmates seem cozy. The monastery was the original penitentiary—a place for doing penance in order to gain the healing of the soul.

The story of St. Mary of Egypt should be familiar to all Orthodox Christians in that it is read aloud, and her life celebrated, during the fifth week of Great Lent each year. The story follows a pattern repeated in various forms in many saints' lives. Mary lived, we think, in the fifth century and began life as a child in Alexandria, Egypt. According to her own witness, she left home as a teen and took up a life of drunkenness and sexual promiscuity. Indeed, we cannot say that she became a prostitute, in that she herself said that what she had done had been largely for pleasure and not for profit. She was the Egyptian version of the "party girl."

One year, she came across what she thought was the beginning of a great party when she encountered a group that was traveling by ship to Palestine to visit Jerusalem for the Feast of the Holy Cross. She had no money, she said, but made her way to the boat, confident that what she would offer would be readily accepted as payment for her passage. She later spoke of corrupting even the young men who were at first unwilling to be her sex partners. Indeed, she said that she continued her activities after the boat had landed and during her first days in the holy city of Jerusalem.

The story changes, however, on the day of the feast. As the crowd was making its way into the Church of the Resurrection, where the Cross was to be displayed, she found herself unable to pass the threshold. It was as though an invisible wall prevented her entrance.

Having repeated my attempt three or four times, at last I felt exhausted and had no more strength to push and to be pushed, so I went aside and stood in a corner of the porch. And only then with great difficulty it began to dawn on me, and I began to understand the reason why I was prevented from being admitted to see the life-giving Cross. The word of salvation gently touched the eyes of my heart and revealed to me that it was my unclean life which barred the entrance to me. I began to weep and lament and beat my breast, and to sigh from the depths of my heart. And so, I stood weeping when I saw above me the icon of the most holy Mother of God. And turning to her . . . I said: "O Lady, Mother of God, who gave birth in the flesh to God the Word, I know, O how well I know, that it is no honor or praise to thee when one so impure and depraved as I look up to thy icon, O ever-virgin, who didst keep thy body and soul in purity. Rightly do I inspire hatred and disgust before thy virginal purity. But I have heard that God Who was born of thee became man on purpose to call sinners to repentance. Then help me, for I have no other help. Order the entrance of the church to be opened to me. Allow me to see the venerable Tree on which He Who was born of thee suffered in the flesh and on which He shed His holy Blood for the redemption of sinners and for me, unworthy as I am. Be my faithful witness before thy son that I will never again defile my body by the impurity of fornication, but as soon as I have seen the Tree of the Cross I will renounce the world and its temptations and will go wherever thou wilt lead me."[17]

Mary's request was granted, after which the Mother of God directed her to the desert. There she lived the rest of her life as a recluse, in prayer and repentance. Toward the end of her life, she encountered the monk Zossima, from whom we have her story. His account includes having seen her raised a foot off the ground in prayer on one occasion and walking on the waters of the Jordan on another. From party girl to penitent to saint, Mary accepted the shame she felt when she was unable to enter the church. From that acceptance, she found the path to the truth of her being. The doors of that church were the gates of paradise.

The paths of repentance followed by St. Mary of Egypt and the criminal-turned-monk described by St. John stand as examples within the monastic world. We find even more extreme examples among those whom the Tradition calls the "holy fools."

---

17 From *The Great Canon, the Work of Saint Andrew of Crete* (Jordanville, NY: Holy Trinity Monastery).

Holy Fools—The Champions of Shame

ALREADY IN THE OLD TESTAMENT, we can see examples of what the Tradition would later describe as "holy foolishness." The Prophet Jeremiah walked through the city of Jerusalem with an ox yoke on his shoulders and only proclaimed his message as a crowd gathered around him. His message was true but unpopular. Indeed, the derision of the crowd alone would have created a state of shame. His outlandish behavior with the ox yoke only pushed matters further.

Saint John the Baptist stands as a bridge between the Old and New Testaments. His prophetic ministry went far beyond his message and included a form of holy foolishness. His manner of clothing (camel hair) and his diet (locusts and wild honey) are among the first things mentioned about him in the Scriptures. His preaching included an invitation to the whole nation to engage in an act of foolishness by submitting to baptism in the Jordan. Time and religious piety have long covered that simple action with praise and admiration. However, initially, it was an act of voluntary humiliation, a public dunking as a sign of turning away from sin.

The examples in Scripture—to which we should add the foolish actions of the followers of Christ, who gave away all they had to follow Him—are clear examples of a willingness to pursue the path of salvation despite the shame that might be involved in those actions. We can easily describe these believers as brave in their foolishness. There are examples beyond those, however, that represent something more, a form of foolishness all its own. These people are named in the Tradition as "holy fools."

These characters are familiar to anyone who studies the Eastern Church in Greece, the Middle East, the Balkans, and Russia. They are men and women who took a path toward holiness in which their apparent foolishness served as a deliberate disguise, even as it was often shocking to the world around them. The Russian writer Sergey Ivanov offers this description of holy fools: "'Holy fool' is a term for a person who feigns insanity, pretends to be silly, or who provokes shock or outrage by his deliberate unruliness."[18]

Reading about their lives can often be entertaining. Piety, in many corners of Christianity, can be highly moralistic and, well, boring. The holy fools destroy such constructs. Saint Simeon of Emesa, often considered the patron saint of holy fools, entered a church and threw nuts at the congregants. Many holy fools went about naked or half-naked. This holy madness included, in Russia, going about undressed and barefoot even in the dead of winter. Saint Basil, the holy fool of Moscow, went about naked, bearing heavy chains. He was known to shoplift in order to feed the poor. He rebuked Tsar Ivan the Terrible to his face—and lived. Saint Xenia of St. Petersburg, after the death of her husband, dressed in his military uniform and refused to answer to anything other than his name.

Two holy fools in Novgorod famously attacked each other. The city had become divided into factions, with those on one side of the river despising and abusing those on the other. Saints Theodore and Nicholas Kochanov (the "Cabbage Head") each took up their positions on either side, in holy mockery of the

---

18 Sergey Ivanov, *Holy Fools in Byzantium and Beyond*, trans. Simon Franklin (Oxford: Oxford University Press, 2005). Kindle loc. 54–55.

public at large. During one battle, when Theodore had crossed into Nicholas's territory, they began to run and fight until St. Theodore ran out onto the river, miraculously followed by St. Nicholas, who was doing the same. Saint Nicholas had grabbed a cabbage head to hurl at St. Theodore, from which he gained his nickname. Whether the story relates exactly what happened is less important than the veneration that accompanied their lives.

Holy fools play an important role in Russian literature and can be found throughout the works of numerous authors, including Pushkin and Dostoevsky. It has even been suggested that Russian culture cannot be fully understood without comprehending the place of the holy fools.[19] I would suggest that Orthodoxy itself cannot be understood apart from holy foolishness. It provides a key insight that pierces into the depths of shame that cover the human heart. Without such an entrance into the depths, there can be no true healing of the soul, nor can the path of the cross be known.

An immunity seems to have been extended to the holy fools by which they could mock church authorities or the tsar himself without being thought of as evil or silenced (though there were certainly plenty of cases in which the authorities pushed back against their actions). This implies a tacit understanding that the greatest of our authorities, whether spiritual or temporal, contain their own hypocrisy. On some level, they deserve to be mocked. If this recognition is lacking, then soon we are

---

19 See Priscilla Hunt, "Holy Foolishness as a Key to Russian Culture," https://slavica.indiana.edu/sites/default/files/bookContent_pdf/Hunt_Kobets_Intro_0.pdf

left with idolatry, worshipping authority rather than merely acknowledging its power.

This kind of critique is even more necessary when we turn our attention toward our own heart. St. Paul declared:

> God has chosen the foolish things of the world to put to shame the wise, and God has chosen the weak things of the world to put to shame the things which are mighty; and the base things of the world and the things which are despised God has chosen, and the things which are not, to bring to nothing the things that are. (1 Cor. 1:27)

In saying this, St. Paul was critiquing the false wisdom, false might, and false existence of the things within ourselves that we enthrone as objects of satisfaction and admiration. As strange as it may seem, these false things are enthroned by our shame and provide cover for the nakedness of our being. It seems to me noteworthy that many of the holy fools were said to have gone naked during much of their ministry. There is likely little else that could adequately clothe such holiness.

Saint Paul's statement is not an isolated comment on his part. Instead, it represents a mature expression within his teaching, consistent with his exposition of the cross and the sacrifice of Christ as well as his understanding of grace and works. Over the years in my ministry, I have come to describe St. Paul's teaching in this manner: We are saved by our weakness, not by our excellence. Discussions of grace versus works quickly bury his insights in religious language such that they easily become obscured or misunderstood. Indeed, contemporary treatments of works and grace often suggest that we are saved in spite of our weakness, with our excellence simply being insufficient. They do not see that excellence itself (or at least the cult of excellence) is problematic. Christian popular culture is as prone to celebrate success as are its secular counterparts. We easily adore the "saints" of cultural competence: the talented, the beautiful, the rich, the lucky. Against this stand the holy fools.

Saint Paul's exaltation of the foolish, the weak, and the nonexistent is nothing novel. He is careful to point toward Christ and the cross itself as the supreme example of foolishness and weakness, just as Christ's death (a seeming failure of cosmic dimensions) is the true victory. Christ teaches that only those who lose their lives will save them. When He identifies Himself with the world, it is with the sick, the naked, the hungry, and the imprisoned (see Matt. 25). Saint Paul's theological treatment of weakness rescues it from the dustbin of morality ("be nice to the poor") and enshrines it as the nature of salvation itself.

Again, our modern handling of weakness in its various forms presents it as unfortunate, as an obstacle that can be overcome through the grace of God. We do not understand it as the gate of paradise. This is utterly contrary to Christ's teaching:

Blessed *are* the poor in spirit,
For theirs is the kingdom of heaven.
Blessed *are* those who mourn,
For they shall be comforted.
Blessed *are* the meek,
For they shall inherit the earth.

Blessed *are* those who hunger and thirst for righteousness,
For they shall be filled.
Blessed *are* the merciful,
For they shall obtain mercy.
Blessed *are* the pure in heart,
For they shall see God.
Blessed *are* the peacemakers,
For they shall be called sons of God.
Blessed *are* those who are persecuted for righteousness'
    sake,
For theirs is the kingdom of heaven. (Matt. 5:3–10)

The mystery of this exaltation of weakness is not found in some perversion of the divine will. Rather, it is found in the perversion of the human heart. It was in shame that we first severed our communion with God, and there seems to be no other way for that broken communion to be healed apart from voluntarily entering that shame. It is for this reason that Christ unites Himself to our shame, becoming poor, meek, hungry, even naked that we might become rich and clothed with the garment of His righteousness. The holy fools serve the purpose of taking such rhetoric away from the lofty sentiments of a theologian and making it concrete and real, to the embarrassment and chagrin of those around them.

It is crucial that we understand that God is not the author of our shame. Our shame flows from our own brokenness and the signals—feelings of inadequacy, abandonment, exposure, and so forth—that accompany the inherent boundaries of our lives. It is only in delusion that we imagine ourselves standing before

God without such boundaries or signals. However, it is when those boundaries and signals, improperly attended to, morph into the deep disease of sin that we begin to imagine them as unbearable and turn toward our shame-created excellence as the false medicine of the soul.

Sergey Ivanov looks outside the bounds of Orthodox Christianity to the role played by clowns and certain forms of shamanism for an even larger display of our human efforts to ameliorate our shame.[20] I noted earlier that laughter, as an emotional expression, eases the pain and discomfort of shame. Humor eases the emotional pain of shame but does not heal its underlying cause. As an emotional medicine, it is effective in the sense that it allows us to acknowledge the reality or presence of our shame and to bear it, to a certain extent. Thus, Scripture says, "A merry heart does good, *like* medicine" (Prov. 17:22). Laughter can also serve as a signal of safety, something we instinctively require in order to bear shame.

Jokes and such are insufficient for the healing of the shame-bound self. They can serve as measures of self-protection (as in the case of the class clown). They do not take us within the shame, much less beneath it. It is beneath that shame, most importantly, that we journey into the true self and the regions that are largely unknown to us.

The holy fools are examples drawn in crayon. They are larger than life, just as their self-imposed shaming is larger than life. At their best, they serve as signs that remind us of the upside-down message of the gospel. It is the poor who become rich, the weak who become strong, the foolish who become wise. That

---

20 Ivanov, *Holy Fools*.

various Orthodox cultures have allowed, even treasured, the presence of holy fools is a testament to the gospel's enculturation within those societies. The same figures, of course, present a puzzlement to those outside those cultures who struggle to understand their occurrences in literature and elsewhere. At the same time, the failure to understand them may represent a tone-deafness to the gospel itself.

Going inside the Fool

THE YEARS FOLLOWING THE FALL of the Soviet Union saw both chaos and discovery in Russia. The collapse of a governing system that sought to dominate every aspect of culture represents far more than a mere political change. Some leaders noted the only institution in that society with a memory that predated the Soviet era was the Orthodox Church. Those who understand Russia best also know that the Orthodox culture of the Church colored many elements of the Soviet world even during its Communist period. The large parades with gigantic portraits of Stalin and Lenin, for example, echoed the great icon processions of important feast days. The grammar of Orthodoxy managed to survive, though the Church was but a shadow of its prerevolutionary self.

I have been a "Russia watcher" since my college years in the 1970s, when Aleksandr Solzhenitsyn's prominence and exile came to international attention. He himself was an Orthodox figure whose conscience whispered of a surviving faith that no amount of persecution could erase. The ability of a society or a culture to produce great literature is a witness to a spiritual presence that might otherwise be overlooked. The West looked at the shards of the Soviet Union and thought mostly about economics and missiles. It failed to ask, "What would be unleashed within the culture itself were the Soviet restraints removed?" That was the question that held my attention.

In 2006, an answer began to emerge. That year, a movie called *The Island* (*Ostrov*) was released. More than that, it won awards in Russia. The film portrayed a monk who was a holy fool living at a monastery on Russia's northern coast. No doubt, he would seem a very odd character to those who knew nothing of Orthodoxy or holy foolishness. However, the film did something new in the depictions of fools: it offered a glimpse into his interior life.

The film opens during the Second World War. The protagonist (whom we will later come to know as Fr. Anatoly) is the mate on a coal ship that has been stopped by a Nazi gunboat. He and the captain seek to hide in a coal pile. However, his cough (which seems incessant throughout the film) gives him away. Under mild physical pressure from the Germans, he gives away the presence of the captain. The tension builds as the German officer gives him a pistol and demands that he shoot his Russian captain, as entertainment for the soldiers. Though he protests and begs for another way, the Germans insist. The Russian captain strikes a pose showing that he despises the whole process. The tension reaches a climax as the young Russian sailor pulls the trigger, watching his captain fall backward into the sea. As the Germans sail away and leave him, he laughs with joy and shouts ridicule in their direction. He has survived—but at what cost? The Germans have left a delayed charge behind. The scene closes with an explosion. We cut to a beach where some monks find a sailor washed up on shore. He will join them and become Fr. Anatoly (he is called "Father" as a monk, though he is not a priest).

The movie shifts forward a number of decades to an aged Fr. Anatoly who is something of a holy fool, believed to be a wonderworker by the local people. What we see, however, is a monk who remains deeply troubled by the sins of his past, who weeps when he prays and always intercedes for the soul of the man he murdered. He indeed has spiritual gifts, but his foolishness serves to hide them. He permits nothing to take away the foolishness and replace it with esteem. For others, he might be a saint. For himself, he is the coward who shot his captain.

The climax of the film comes when a retired Soviet admiral brings his daughter to Fr. Anatoly for healing. Anatoly tells him that his daughter is possessed by a demon. The man is put off by such a diagnosis but is unable to take his daughter away. For Fr. Anatoly, the encounter is beyond profound, for the admiral is none other than the boat captain whom he thought he had killed. At his greeting he says, "Angels are singing in my soul!" He successfully drives the demon from the man's daughter. Sometime later, we see Fr. Anatoly peacefully end his days as he lies in a coffin that he had requested be built for him.

His holy foolishness is part of his repentance, a lifetime of intercession for the man he assumed he had murdered. Though he has gained a measure of renown through the grace given to him, only his madness (foolishness) protects him from neglecting the seriousness of the soul-sickness that allowed him to kill in such a cowardly manner. The admiral's appearance is a lifetime's answered prayer.

When I first saw this film, I was astounded that such a work of art had been made. It was something Hollywood could not have imagined. It was as authentic and creative as it was brilliant. Over time, *The Island* has become extremely popular across the Orthodox world.

In 2012, a novel by a Russian author, Eugene Vodolazkin, appeared in Russia. It was translated and published in English in 2015. The novel, *Laurus*, quickly took its place within the substantial literature of Orthodoxy. The book is set in Russia's medieval period and follows a man who becomes a holy fool. The novel does what official saints' lives do not do and what the film *The Island* could only do in part: it gives us the deep thoughts and inner workings of the heart of a holy fool. We see the protagonist's response to the shame engendered by his causing the needless death of a woman called Ustina, who had lived with our protagonist (then called Arseny), and her newborn child, whom he had fathered. The shame is mingled with his deep grief. Early on, he is utterly shut down in his grief, slowly moving toward his own death. A holy elder from a nearby monastery intervenes and shows a way forward:

> I know you are dreaming about death. You are thinking death now possesses everything you held dear. But you are wrong. Death does not possess Ustina. Death is only carrying her to Him Who will administer justice over her. And thus, even if you decide now to give yourself to Death, you will not be united with Ustina. . . .
>
> I will not pity you: you are to blame for her bodily death. You are also to blame that her soul may perish. I

should have said that beyond the grave it is already too late to save her life, but you know what, I will not say that. Because there is no already where she is now. And there is no still. And there is no time, though there is God's eternal mercy, we trust in His mercy. But mercy should be a reward for effort. . . . You have a difficult journey, for the story of your love is only beginning. Everything, O Arseny, will now depend on the strength of your love. And, of course, on the strength of your prayers, too.[21]

Arseny begins a journey. For some time he answers only to the name Ustin. Eventually he will become Amvrosy and ultimately Laurus. In the course of a lifetime that includes a pilgrimage to the Holy Land, he presses ever deeper beneath the shame. His progressive change of name reflects a movement through his shame as well as a movement into the depths of holiness. His inner dialogue is a voice that appears throughout the novel. He never forgets Ustina, the woman who died because he was ashamed to acknowledge her and take her as his wife. But like Fr. Anatoly in *The Island*, his foolishness brings him to a place of redemption.

For Laurus, redemption comes as he shelters a young pregnant woman in his hermit cave. However, he does not hide her as he did Ustina. Instead, although he is innocent, he accepts blame and responsibility for her condition without complaint. At the end of his life, he safely delivers her child and dies as he sits holding him in his arms. His final disposition follows his request:

21 Eugene Vodolazkin, *Laurus*, trans. Lisa C. Hayden (One World Publications, 2015), 90–91.

You know, I have a favor to ask, too. When I leave my body, do not be very ceremonious with it, for I have, after all, synned [sinned] with it. Tie a rope to the legs and drag it into the swampy wilds for the animals and vipers to tear to pieces. That's basically it.[22]

True to himself as a fool, his nonburial is that of a fool as well.

It is significant that such literary characters exist. Indeed, many of the stories and exploits attributed to Laurus in the novel are drawn from the lives of famous holy fools in Russia and elsewhere. He is something of a composite fool.

Shame is called by many therapists the "unbearable emotion." In the stories of the holy fools, we see that shame can not only be borne, it can even be embraced. It is a very difficult, even bitter, medicine, but so is the disease that such foolishness seeks to treat. The disease is the life of a false self, in which every kind of passion is indulged and our false identities lead us on a dance that dares not speak its name or acknowledge its reality.

What we learn from these stories is that there is a path toward God and the authentic soul or self. That path has the character of foolishness and draws us inevitably toward a shame we might otherwise seek to avoid. It is, however, the voice of paradise itself that calls us back to the truth of our being and the nakedness of our soul. Our next chapter will look at some of the dynamics of this process and the ministry that surrounds it.

---

22 Vodolazkin, *Laurus*, 356.

CHAPTER FIVE

Confession: Speaking the Truth in Love

I STILL HATE GOING TO CONFESSION."
That admission from the late Archbishop Dmitri of Dallas came as a great surprise to me. We were having a casual conversation about a range of topics. At some point the subject of confession came up, and he made this striking statement. He was a man whom many here in the South consider to be a modern saint. That fact makes his statement all the more poignant. Why would a senior cleric, a man of great holiness, "hate" confession? He did not expound on the statement, though I think I understood. He "hated" confession *because he had learned how to confess.* When St. Sophrony prepared the younger priestmonks in his monastery to begin hearing confessions, his instructions to them were to teach those making confession "how to bear a little shame." This advice goes to the heart of confession and brings to light the medicine it provides to the wounded soul.

Private confession is something many people have only seen in the movies or learned to do as a child. The movies are often less than helpful, driven as they are by Hollywood's abysmal and caricatured understanding of Christianity.

Various prayer books and manuals offer directions for confession, some providing lists of sins to use in an examination of conscience. Often, the effect of the examples and directives people see is to point them toward a legal or *transactional* understanding of the sacrament:

» I did something wrong.
» I deserve punishment.
» I confess my sins and promise to do better.
» God forgives me.

This raises all sorts of questions. What if I leave out a sin? How often should I confess? If I have committed a sin after confession, can I still take communion? Such questions, particularly for those with a fastidious conscience, easily multiply.

In another conversation with Archbishop Dmitri, I asked him about those who rarely come to confession or, when they come, say they aren't aware of any sins. His instructions were enlightening: "If they can do nothing more than say to God, 'I am a sinner,' then give them absolution and welcome them to communion." This, of course, was not meant as an example of a model confession, but it reveals the heart of the sacrament.

I can easily imagine a situation in which one individual describes a list of sins while another merely says "I am a sinner," and the second receives significant healing while the first walks away unchanged. How is this possible? If confession were a legal, transactional matter, then forgiveness would be external, a wiping clean of a legal slate ("all charges have been dropped"). However, the sacraments and life of the Church are more accurately understood in a medical model. What truly takes place within the soul reveals the nature of the sacrament. Thus, it is more important to ask in the sacrament, "What is the state of my heart?"

I recall one evening in the church as I sat waiting for people to come up for confession. At a certain point, I noticed someone approaching, weeping and wiping away tears. My thought at the time was that the confession was already taking place. A heart was already standing naked before God. The person certainly needed the sacrament to be fulfilled; indeed, I think it was the looming reality of revealing the heart out loud that provoked the tears. That experience brought to mind the verse from the Psalms: "A broken and contrite heart—these, O God, You will not despise" (Ps. 50/51:17).

It is this state of the heart in the sacrament that St. Sophrony had in mind when he advised, "Teach them to bear a little shame." Our sin represents our hiding from God, an effort to live in a shameless manner (where a little shame would be more natural, honest, and healthy). Confession is an essential part of the life of repentance, in which we seek to live in true union with God, face-to-face, even when it requires that we endure some shame.

An interesting story from the Desert Fathers illustrates an exceedingly merciful approach to sin with a focus on the heart:

On one occasion Abba Ammon came to a certain place to eat with the brothers, and there was there a brother concerning whom evil reports were abroad, for it had happened that a woman had come and entered his cell. And when all the people who were living in that place heard [of this], they were troubled, and they gathered together to expel that brother from his cell, and learning that the blessed Bishop Ammon was there, they came and entreated him to go with them. Now when the brother knew [this], he took the woman and hid her under an earthenware vessel. A crowd having assembled, and Abba Ammon, understanding what that brother had done, for the sake of God, hid the matter. And he went in and sat upon the earthenware vessel, and commanded that the cell of the brother should be searched, but although they examined the place they found no one there. Then Abba Ammon answered and said, 'What is this that you have done? May God forgive you'; and he prayed and said, 'Let all the people go forth,' and finally he took the brother by the hand, and said to him, 'Take heed to your soul, O my brother,' and having said this he departed, and he refused to make public the matter of the brother.[23]

It would have been possible in this situation to judge the erring brother from a legal standpoint. He was guilty of an infraction of the rule (the story discreetly abstains from describing any wrongdoing with the woman). In terms of guilt, he would have been deserving of whatever punishment came his way. As Abba Ammon sat on the lid of the earthenware vessel, he actively covered the sin of the young monk. He not only refused to disclose the sin but deliberately hid it. His admonition, "Take

---

23 Palladius, *The Sayings of the Holy Desert Fathers*, trans. E. A. Wallis Budge (Christian Classics, 2016), IX, 400.

heed to your soul, O my brother," served not as a legal remedy (indeed, "legal remedy" is an oxymoron) but as a medicinal balm to the soul.

It is worth pondering the dynamic of shame in this setting. The brother hides the woman in the vessel, even as Adam and Eve sought to hide themselves from God. He has broken communion with the brotherhood (and with God). The abba, however, does not seek to expose him to a greater shame, a shame that would destroy him. Instead, by covering the brother's shame, he acknowledges that he himself sees the truth of what has taken place, and in so doing, he shows the truth to the monk. His words pointing the monk to his soul are a directive of healing, for it is only in taking heed to his soul that the monk can become who he is truly meant to be.

This story could be taken as a model of the sacrament of confession. In one of the traditional introductory prayers for confession, the priest offers this admonition:

> Behold, my child, Christ stands here invisibly and receives your confession. Wherefore be not ashamed or afraid and conceal nothing from me but tell without hesitation all things which you have done, and so you shall have pardon from our Lord Jesus Christ. Lo, His holy image is before us, and I am but a witness, bearing testimony before Him of the things which you have to say. But if you shall conceal anything you shall have the greater sin. Take heed, therefore, lest having come to the physician, you depart unhealed.

The priest claims no particular power for himself. A mystical healing of the soul is offered:

> Do not conceal even one sin, not even because of shame, for I also am a man subject to passions, able to fall into similar sins, and I have experience of the weakness of man. And when despising the shame which you shall expose to the One God, through me, you will not be accused of these sins before the Angels of God and before all men at the dread Judgement. . . . Do not hide anything because of infirmity, for I will not be angry at you, neither will I make public your sins; but I will heal you with gentleness of soul. And when you confess, expose everything, and I will not censure you; uncover your sins, and I will not be as a stranger to you. . . . Having ordered your heart, give glory to the Lord.[24]

It is clear that no *transaction* is taking place. Shame seems to be the operative issue. The penitent is encouraged to "despise the shame"—meaning to ignore it and go forward—and to "expose" her sins before God.

> Confessing your transgressions before me, a sinner, and receiving absolution, you will be freed from the bonds of sins, you will be cleansed, and you will be healed spiritually by the grace of God.[25]

---

24 *The Great Book of Needs*, Vol. 1 (South Canaan, PA: St. Tikhon's Seminary Press, 1998), 123.
25 Ibid.

The mystery of confession turns on the problem of shame, both in its presence within us and in its healing. We are encouraged not to hide, which is shame's most immediate instinct, but to bring ourselves visibly into the presence of God, with a witness. The goal is both to see ourselves as we truly are and to see God as He truly is. In truth, this is an exercise with layers upon layers of reality. Our vision of ourselves is often distorted and inaccurate, as is our vision of God. The presence of a witness (the priest) can often be of assistance in clarifying these distortions. In the Scriptures, learning to see is often the same thing as learning to know. Knowledge of the self, like the knowledge of God, is perhaps the most difficult knowledge of all.

Classical Greek mythology contains a story about a beautiful young man, Narcissus. He seems incapable of loving any other person for the simple reason that he sees no one as beautiful as himself. As a punishment from the gods, he becomes lost and frozen as he looks at his own image reflected in a pool of water. He dies in this state and is replaced with the flower that bears his name. In our own time, his name has been given to the mental illness of narcissism—the dark fascination with our own selves.

Some have applied this term to our fascination with selfies, the many pictures of ourselves posted in social media. I have long pondered the question of why selfies are so attractive. We have an age-old love affair with our own images—witness the use of mirrors or the painting of portraits. It is possible, of course, to stand back and condemn the culture of selfies as just another form of narcissism. It is more helpful, however, to think more carefully about the dynamic that is taking place.

I think the fascination with the image of the self means that we are looking for something essential to our well-being, centering in the question, "Who am I?" This is instructive in that shame is the emotion associated with how we feel about who we are. Our fascination, I believe, is an effort to attend to the shame that accompanies our thoughts of self. "If I *look* OK, then maybe I *am* OK."

Confession brings us face to face with our shame, but in a different manner. Confession is not a selfie that seeks to say all is well. It is a self-exposure that we would likely never want to see posted online. It is also a revelation of the face of Christ that can be found in no other way. In our imaginations, we hide our sin and the selves we imagine ourselves to be, lest we face what we believe to be condemnation from Christ. And here, confession is critical to our knowledge of God and the self. We do not find Christ condemning us or despising us. This, in my experience, is an extremely important aspect of the sacrament.

We may be tempted to treat confession as an exercise in moral husbandry, that is, an occasion for making people behave. Sadly, this can leave the soul damaged, because it confuses God with a strict parental figure. We cannot love if we do not know that we ourselves are loved. We cannot forgive until we know ourselves to be forgiven. The *Odes of Solomon*, an early Christian document, says:

> Behold, our mirror is the Lord;
> Open (your) eyes and see them in Him.

And learn the manner of your face.
Then announce praises to His Spirit.[26]

This idea is also found in the New Testament and later in the Fathers, particularly in St. Gregory of Nyssa. In Christ we see the face of God. What is the content of that face? If we scan the Gospels for what they say of Christ, we find the beginnings of a proper guide to what we should see. The Gospels give numerous examples of how Christ responds to those who come to Him with their sins. Consistently, we find a gentle acceptance and a word of forgiveness. In numerous cases, He simply pronounces sins to be forgiven when not a word of confession or repentance has been uttered. This is sometimes connected with the healing of a physical disease.

My favorite example in this vein is the encounter between Christ and the woman taken in adultery (John 8). She is brought before Him by the scribes and Pharisees, who say that she has been caught "in the very act." Thus, there is no question of her guilt. Their question to Christ concerns her punishment. The Law of Moses demands that she be stoned. Famously, Christ responds, "Whoever is without sin, let him cast the first stone." They walk away, perhaps disappointed.

Christ then speaks to the woman, saying, "Where are your accusers? Has no one condemned you?"

She replies, "No one, Lord."

Christ—the only one without sin—says to her, "Neither do I condemn you. Go, and sin no more."

---

26 Odes of Solomon, 13. *The Earliest Christian Hymnbook*, trans. James H. Charlesworth (Eugene, OR: Cascade Books, 2009), 77.

This example concerns a major sin, something that later centuries will categorize with theft and murder. So much of this story is simply unspoken. We are given no information about the history of this woman nor of what is taking place within her. We are left to assume that all this is known to Christ as God. What we see, though, is the astonishing effect of this encounter: *she is not condemned.* Her being sent away with the words "Go, and sin no more" also indicates that she has been *healed*—she is no longer in the grip or power of that sin. She is free.

Fr. Alexander Schmemann taught that, in the sacraments, Christ does not make something to be what it is not, but reveals something to be what it truly is.[27] Thus bread, in the sacrament of the Eucharist, is revealed in its truest intention and existence: it is given to us for communion with God. This teaching is consistent with the Orthodox understanding of salvation itself. Sin interrupts the life of communion and perverts the proper direction of our existence. *Theosis*, or divinization, has always been the intention of God for our lives. As St. Gregory of Nyssa is quoted as saying, "Man is mud who has been commanded to become a god." The sacrament of confession is above all an encounter with the risen Christ that restores us to the proper trajectory of our life. In His presence, sin is revealed. But greater than that, the truth of ourselves is revealed and restored. In His presence, we become what we were created to be. As St. John writes:

---

27 Alexander Schmemann, *For the Life of the World*, SVSP Classics Series, vol. 1 (Crestwood, NY: St. Vladimir's Seminary Press, 2018), 143.

Beloved, now we are children of God; and it has not yet been revealed what we shall be, but we know that when He is revealed, we shall be like Him, for we shall see Him as He is. And everyone who has this hope in Him purifies himself, just as He is pure. (1 John 3:2–3)

This in many ways sets the parameters for the ministry of a confessor. The essential work of the gospel is to present Christ to the world and the world to Christ.

The writer of the *Odes of Solomon* is correct: "Our mirror is the Lord." We look on Him in order to see the manner of our own face.

The Mirror of St. Paul

IN TWO SEPARATE PASSAGES, ST. Paul makes use of the image of a mirror. Both passages are focused on the face of Christ: "For now, we see in a mirror, dimly, but then face to face. Now I know in part, but then I shall know just as I also am known" (1 Cor. 13:12). And "But we all, with unveiled face, beholding as in a mirror the glory of the Lord, are being transformed into the same image from glory to glory, just as by the Spirit of the Lord" (2 Cor. 3:18). He also gives us this clarification: "For it is the God who commanded light to shine out of darkness, who has shone in our hearts to *give* the light of the knowledge of the glory of God in the face of Jesus Christ" (2 Cor. 4:6).

We also have this saying from Christ: "The lamp of the body is the eye. If therefore your eye is single [whole], your whole body will be full of light. But if your eye is bad, your whole body will be full of darkness. If therefore the light that is in you is darkness, how great is that darkness!" (Matt. 6:22).

In human experience, nothing seems more important than the face. It is the canvas where we display our emotions. It is the primary means by which we identify one another. It is both how we know and how we are known. It is the place where we most prominently experience shame. Indeed, we speak of the "face of shame," being "shamefaced," and of "losing face." It is significant in this respect that we are directed to look at an icon of Christ as we make confession: we see Him face to face. This also provokes shame to some small degree, as it should. To a certain extent, this shame is a softening of the heart, an exercise in humility, also known as healthy shame.

It seems critical to me that this face-to-face encounter with Christ take place in accordance with the truth. I recall a story shared by a friend. My friend was in conversation (not confession) with a priest about God. As they spoke, my friend described God's disapproval and rather stern aspect. The priest had on his desk the icon called "Extreme Humility," which depicts Christ in His suffering and humiliation. He turned the icon around so my friend could see it. The priest said, "Which God are we talking about?" An immediate clarity came to my friend, who realized that the image of God in his mind had been a false image.

Christ said, "Come to Me, all *you* who labor and are heavy laden, and I will give you rest. Take My yoke upon you and learn from Me, for I am gentle and lowly in heart, and you will find rest for your souls. For My yoke is easy and My burden is light" (Matt. 11:28–30). This text is commonly displayed on the open pages of a Gospel book in the icon of Christ the

Almighty (Pantokrator). Though many describe that icon as "stern," it merely intends to present Him as all-powerful. The text of the Gospel conveys the full intention ("gentle and lowly in heart").

This points to a larger question in the life of the Church. The whole of what we do and of what we say in our liturgies and prayers is grounded in the Church's knowledge of Christ. At its deepest level, this is the heart of Orthodoxy. Though the word "Orthodoxy" in English is sometimes translated "right teaching," its more literal meaning is "right worship." This comes to a point of dynamic importance in the face-to-face encounter of confession.

Culturally, it is easy to fall into a distortion of confession in which it becomes an exercise in moral management—the effort of a pastor to manage, even control, the behavior of his congregation. The goal of his efforts may be a kind of moral conformity, the performance of a correct prayer rule, careful observance of the fasting rules, and so forth. Depending on many factors in an individual life, such an approach can yield almost the opposite of its desired intention.

Christ says, "A good man out of the good treasure of his heart brings forth good; and an evil man out of the evil treasure of his heart brings forth evil. For out of the abundance of the heart his mouth speaks" (Luke 6:45). Mere conformity to a moral standard can leave the heart untouched. Christ's struggle with the Pharisees seemed to turn precisely on this point. He warned His followers that though they should do what they heard the Pharisees say, they should strive not to do as those hypocrites actually did. He described them as "whitewashed tombs which indeed appear beautiful outwardly, but inside are full of dead *men's* bones and all uncleanness" (Matt. 23:27).

This false idealization of an outward moral standard is but one among many delusions we may encounter in the spiritual life. It is equally easy for us to mistake our own neurosis, the inner dance with the passions, for God Himself. The "inner voice" that many ascribe to God is frequently nothing of the sort. The practice of confession, in which we bring our hidden things out of the darkness and into the light, can be a safeguard against the many mistaken paths we choose for ourselves. Discernment on the part of a wise confessor can be instrumental in helping us find our way forward.

All that should be coupled with patience. There are no infallible confessors, no all-wise guides for the soul. We sometimes go two steps forward and one step back, or worse. The goal, above all else, is to stand spiritually naked before God, to see ourselves as we are revealed in Him, without pretense, without excuse. At the same time, the goal for a confessor is to consistently teach and present the love of God above all things, that others might come to know Him as He is revealed in the face of Jesus Christ.

As a final note, we can say that we will not know God more clearly than we know ourselves, and that we will not know ourselves more clearly than we know God. These two types of imaging are indissolubly linked. The moral guide in our life, the path toward true holiness, is consistently pointed out by Christ in His admonitions for us to be like God. He is our life.

"Love your enemies, do good to those who hate you, bless those who curse you, and pray for those who spitefully use you. To him who strikes you on the *one* cheek, offer the other also. And from him who takes away your cloak, do not withhold *your* tunic either. Give to everyone who asks of you. And from him who takes away your goods do not ask *them* back. And just as you want men to do to you, you also do to them likewise.

"But if you love those who love you, what credit is that to you? For even sinners love those who love them. And if you do good to those who do good to you, what credit is that to you? For even sinners do the same. And if you lend *to those* from whom you hope to receive back, what credit is that to you? For even sinners lend to sinners to receive as much back. But love your enemies, do good, and lend, hoping for nothing in return; and your reward will be great, and you will be sons of the Most High. For He is kind to the unthankful and evil. Therefore, be merciful, just as your Father also is merciful." (Luke 6:27–36)

CHAPTER SIX

Shame, Envy and Pride: A Dark Story

A LOCAL CONVERSATION here in East Tennessee:
"Who's your favorite team?"
"Tennessee, and anybody playing Alabama."

College football is a big thing in the South. People who live in the cities where major sports programs are located become accustomed to the team colors and mascot being present almost everywhere. When the local team does well, a general sense of well-being pervades the community. When it does poorly, people are disgruntled and easily provoked.

Sports teams and fandom are nothing new. Ancient Rome had its teams of chariot racers, the Blues and the Greens. In AD 532, Blues and Greens fans in Constantinople broke into rioting. They burned the church that was the precursor to Hagia Sophia and eventually sought to overthrow the emperor. Things came to a head during one of the chariot races in the Hippodrome. The stadium could hold 150,000. At a signal, the emperor's troops entered the stadium and began to slaughter both Blues and Greens. When the day ended, contemporary historians relate that around 30,000 had been killed. Sports can be a serious business.

It's an interesting phenomenon. Year after year, riots and deaths surround sporting occasions throughout the world. Of course, when examined from a dispassionate angle, the outcome of a sporting match is of no consequence. It is only a game. Examined from a passionate angle, however, it can be a matter of life and death. The passion involved is largely that of shame, but it also includes its dark cousin, envy. Together these two explain a wide range of human history, as well as some of the most powerful dark energies of our private lives. Shame and envy have an interrelationship that is worth exploring, particularly if we want to see the face of God in its truth.

Shame and Envy

IN POPULAR USAGE, THE TERM envy is seen as synonymous with jealousy or covetousness. As such, it describes how we feel about the good fortune of others. The word, however, has a darker history. A definition that some dictionaries now describe as "obsolete" reveals that it once carried the sense of malice as well. We not only wish we had someone else's good fortune, but we also take pleasure in their misfortune. This older meaning is captured well in a statement of Aristotle's: "Envy is pain at the good fortune of others" (*Rhetoric*, Book II, Chapter 10). Immanuel Kant offers a similar sentiment: "[Envy] aims, at least in terms of one's wishes, at destroying others' good fortune" (*The Metaphysics of Morals*, 6:459). It is this older, darker meaning of the word that I have in mind in this chapter. It is, perhaps, a pity that modern English usage seems to have no common word for this ever-so-common human feeling. We often borrow the German equivalent, *schadenfreude.*

Some of the Church Fathers saw in envy the darkest and most dangerous of all sins. Saint Gregory of Nyssa wrote:

> Envy is the passion which causes evil, the father of death, the first entrance of sin, the root of wickedness, the birth of sorrow, the mother of misfortune, the basis of disobedience, the beginning of shame. Envy banished us from Paradise, having become a serpent to oppose Eve. Envy walled us off from the tree of life, divested us of holy garments, and in shame led us away clothed with fig leaves. Envy armed Cain contrary to nature and instituted the death which is vindicated seven times. Envy made Joseph a slave. Envy is the death-dealing sting, the hidden weapon, the sickness of nature, the bitter poison, the self-willed emaciation, the bitter dart, the nail of the soul, the fire in the heart, the flame burning on the inside.[28]

This older meaning of envy, sometimes called "malicious envy," can be described as the joy or satisfaction we feel at the misfortune of others. When your team wins, you take pleasure in it; well and good. When the rival team loses and you find pleasure in it, envy is at work. Our reactions to sporting events may be inconsequential; more insidious is the envy that stalks our lives

---

28 Cited by J. Farrugia (2021), "Insights on hatred, envy and hypocrisy in Gregory of Nyssa's homilies," *Academia Letters*, Article 782. https://doi.org/10.20935/AL782.

in our mundane activities. "He had it coming to him" is the often unspoken voice of envy.

In the ancient world, and even today along the Mediterranean rim, there is a common folk belief in the "evil eye." Explanations for this cultural phenomenon abound. At its heart it represents the fear of envy and the danger it brings. Beyond the superstitions associated with the evil eye (such as wearing or displaying amulets of protection), the Tradition provides a more sober recognition of the threat of envy. This is particularly true in the prayers surrounding the birth of a child.[29]

The persistence over so many centuries of concern about malicious envy points to a deeper, darker meaning than the more common characterization of envy. To debate whether envy can project trouble with nothing more than a look is a distraction from the real point. To look at another with a heart darkened by envy is, at the very least, a prelude to trouble. Living with people who wish you harm or who would rejoice if harm came your way is a dangerous existence.

Wars, murders, and lesser forms of mischief have their roots in the heart. Tragically, history books attribute conflicts like war to larger problems such as economics, politics, or vague historical forces. Such realities, however, are carried out by collectives of individuals in whose hearts are the seedbed of all human conflict. There is a reason soldiers invariably create nicknames for their adversaries. It is ever so much easier to kill a cartoon character out of history than your actual cousin

---

29 Fr. George Aquaro has done an interesting study on this topic. See his *Death by Envy: The Evil Eye and Envy in the Christian Tradition* (New York: iUniverse, Inc., 2004).

(during World War I, for instance, the crowned heads of Britain and Germany were first cousins). Many of the lasting ethnic hatreds across the world have their origins in the envious images of earlier wars.

The story of the first murder is a story of envy. In Genesis we read the story of Cain and Abel, the sons of Adam and Eve. They offer sacrifices to God. Cain, the farmer, makes an offering from the fruit of his fields. Abel, a herdsman, offered from his animals. With no explanation (in the Hebrew text), we are told that God "had regard" for the sacrifice of Abel but not for that of Cain. And then shame entered the picture. We are told that Cain's "countenance fell"—that is, he was shamed by God's response. That shame, in the form of envy, was turned toward Abel, whom Cain killed shortly afterward.

This pattern, in which shame transforms into envy, is quite common and is likely the primary source of envy.[30] We have seen that shame is the "master emotion." It is also painful, and it frequently morphs and expresses itself as a secondary emotion. We can trace the transformation of shame into envy simply by following the movements within our own hearts. In shame we feel exposed. Simple comparisons to others and their perceived success or excellence can easily provoke our own sense of inadequacy or failure. The entire panoply of shame-inducing experiences—unrequited love, exclusion, unwanted exposure, disappointed expectation, and so forth—particularly when compared with those whose situation seems preferable to our

---

30 A brief discussion and example of this shame-envy relationship can be found in an article by Joseph Burgo, "Shame and How It Produces Envy," http://www.afterpsychotherapy.com/shame-and-envy/

own, provide a ready seedbed for feelings of envy. The other's success increases the pain and burden of our shame. Sadly, we often feel a certain relief from that burden when a misfortune comes their way. It brings with it a distorted sense of pleasure.

Consider a hypothetical scenario: A teen in school sees another child as a rival. The rival excels in precisely the areas where the first child feels inadequate. The rival is liked by another in the class that the first child wishes to be liked by. The first child feels excluded by the popularity of his rival. In the presence of the rival he feels embarrassed and exposed, constantly disappointed in his own desires. As a result, those feelings of shame become feelings of envy. The envy emerges in an occasional conversation in which the rival is portrayed in a bad light. Envy breeds gossip. In our world, such gossip can quickly enter the realm of social media and become a source of pain. One child's envy can drive another child to thoughts of suicide. Such stories are the stuff of teen movies—and the movies work because they are a reflection of a very widespread experience.

That teenage scenario can easily be transferred to the workplace, or a church community, or any social setting. Unresolved shame is a breeding ground for envy. Envy is the breeding ground for much darker passions: lies, slander, gossip, even murder. Christ said, "The lamp of the body is the eye. If therefore your eye is good, your whole body will be full of light. But if your eye is bad, your whole body will be full of darkness. If therefore the light that is in you is darkness, how great is that darkness!" (Matt. 6:22).

It is striking that in the Greek, the phrase "if your eye is bad" means literally "if your eye is evil." Shame darkens our "eyes" or perceptions, coloring the world around us. It becomes a source of envy in which we become bearers of the "evil eye," not in the sense of anything magical, but in the sense that we delight in the misfortune of others and are even drawn into settings in which we contribute to their misfortune. If gossip or slander has been a problem in your life, chances are that you are living with unresolved shame and have been living with a heart that harbors envy. Christ warns, "If the light that is in you is darkness, how great is that darkness!" We experience that darkness as anxiety, anger, moodiness, sadness, and a host of other miseries.

Public life in the modern world is deeply shaped by shame and envy. In a highly commercialized culture, customers are most easily gained through the arousal of emotions. Simply getting people to think or to rationally consider the pros and cons of a matter or a purchase is far too risky for the business of marketing. Emotional responses are more predictable and effective. A British documentary, *The Century of the Self* (2002), is one of the most in-depth and accessible treatments of the role of the manipulation of various emotions in modern advertising. Through interviews and historical documents, it traces the marriage of psychology and marketing that has shaped the world of advertising as well as politics. The one missing element, I would suggest, is its failure to analyze the place of shame in that mix.

We may easily observe that human beings desire certain things. What is not often asked is *why* we desire them. Often, the answer is that we think these things will make the inner aches and pains brought about by unattended shame go away or at least lessen. For instance, the 1950s famously saw striking cosmetic changes in the appearance of American automobiles each year. These changes had no practical advantage. They were made solely for the purpose of change in accordance with a marketing strategy that nurtured the shameful feeling of having an older car. As with fashions in clothing, nothing more is needed than to make what is entirely adequate (last year's style) feel inadequate this year. Only shame, the emptiness that comes from the sense of not belonging, serves the emotional requirements for such a strategy. We market with an eye to creating shame.

Were these public manipulations merely about buying and selling, they would seem innocuous. However, the same marketing energies that make a dress seem hopelessly out of date are, in more sophisticated forms, equally useful in creating political movements and marketing candidates for public office. The most common strategies in these public offerings are built on both shame and envy. These two emotions are substantive bonds in combining a sense of belonging with a sense of perceived danger. Thus, our public life has become highly polarized, with each side seeing the other as a threat while their own side alone is safe, sane, and correct. Shame and envy flourish.

Pride

IN HIS *PURGATORIO*, DANTE PLACED the sin of pride as the worst of sins, followed closely by envy. In truth, envy and pride tend to be enmeshed in one another, particularly through their roots in shame. If one aspect of shame is its declaration of "how I feel about who I am," then it is easy to see this relationship between envy and pride. If the flourishing of someone else can provoke shame in me and give rise to envy, then, by the same token, my own flourishing can provide a shield against shame and manifest itself as an inordinate pride. Both envy and pride are rooted in relationship, in how I see myself in comparison to others.

The term translated as "pride" in Orthodox Tradition is the Greek *philautia*—literally, "love of self." It does not mean a proper concern for the self but a love and concern for the self that is broken off and independent of our relations with others. For example, we cannot see ourselves accurately simply by looking at ourselves. The soul does not serve as a private mirror. Who and what we are is the product of those who have gone before us as well as those who are all around us, including God. We do not exist as a self-generated identity. The love of self that we designate as pride is a distorted self-above-all. Shame plays the major role in its creation.

The rupture in communion created by the experience of shame is painful. Rather than enduring the pain and attending to the rupture, we turn to the self and rush to its protection. Shielding the self from shame, however, can foster even greater problems. Since shame is unavoidable in the course of a normal life, strategies that seek to avoid it or to shield us from it become problems in themselves. Everything from social anxiety to addiction can have roots in the effort to avoid shame and protect the self. False pride, in which the self becomes grandiose and inflated, is another strategy to avoid shame. More clinical and destructive is the syndrome of narcissism, in which a self seems utterly unable to handle any amount of shame.

At their heart, our lives consist of a balancing act between our own needs and the legitimate needs of others. In a healthy

situation, that balancing begins very early in life. The psalmist
says:

> Lord, my heart is not haughty,
> Nor my eyes lofty.
> Neither do I concern myself with great matters,
> Nor with things too profound for me.
> Surely, I have calmed and quieted my soul,
> Like a weaned child with his mother;
> Like a weaned child *is* my soul within me.
> O Israel, hope in the Lord
> From this time forth and forever. (Psalm 131)

The beginning of the psalm frames its context. The writer
resists the temptation of pride ("my heart is not haughty"). He
is not wrongly concerned with things that are "too profound."
He is able to accept the "healthy shame" of his actual position within the world. He acknowledges God and directs his
conversation toward Him. He compares his soul to that of a
weaned child. This is a child that has successfully been separated from its mother. The natural narcissism of a child's earliest existence, in which the world seems to exist only to meet
the child's needs, has been outgrown and replaced with the
ability to calm and quiet the soul in a healthy relationship with
its mother. The child has not outgrown a need for its mother,
but the mother now has an existence that is greater than, or
separate from, the child itself. This is the model of balance. We
have our own legitimate needs that must be balanced with the
legitimate needs that surround us.

That the psalmist turns to childhood for an illustration of this peaceful and healthy existence is deeply insightful, for it is in these early years of life that the foundation of later health is created. We continue throughout our lives to work at this inner balance. It can be crippling, however, if damage is done to the soul when we are young. Contemporary psychological terminology speaks about the "self-esteem" of a child, language which some Christians react to as though it were encouraging an unhealthy pride or self-centeredness. When the term is unpacked, however, it can be seen as an attempt to describe the ability of a child to be self-comforting in situations of social stress. In the language of this book, I would describe self-esteem as the ability of a child to weather moments of healthy shame without becoming too distraught, anxious, or sad. Classically, this can be understood as the underpinnings of humility. It is instructive that this psalm is framed in terms of humility. We do not, of course, place adult expectations on a child. The psalmist, however, has mastered some of the most profound skills of the inner life.

Love of Enemy

ENVY AND PRIDE, DESPITE OUR best intentions, always threaten our relationships with others. Nowhere is this more true than in those situations in which we confront our enemies. Christ does not avoid this painful reality but draws our attention to it directly, commanding, "Love your enemies" (Matt. 5:44).

In general, we instinctively seek to put a boundary between ourselves and our enemies and often enough direct a fair amount of envy toward them, wishing them harm. Those who might wish us harm (both physically and otherwise) could properly be described as enemies. How are we to love them?

I recall my wife describing a scene of Muhammed Ali, the boxer, meeting with a group of children. A young boy of age four or five wanted to box with the champ. Ali obliged him by playfully parrying his small swings, until at last he let one through and fell down. The boy was thrilled, to say the least. Ali, for his part, was all smiles. He was not threatened or shamed, nor did he see himself diminished in any way. This, my wife said, was true humility. Nothing about the great boxer was on the line that day other than his kindness and his patience. His healthy and natural pride was not damaged.

Humility is not a virtue in which we think less of ourselves, as in self-denigration. Rather, humility is a strength of the self, an ability to bear our own healthy shame. It allows us to see the excellence and strength of others and not be threatened or shamed. Our well-being does not require the misfortune of others.

Christ points to the example of God when he teaches us about care for our enemies:

"But I say to you, love your enemies, bless those who curse you, do good to those who hate you, and pray for those who spitefully use you and persecute you, that you may be sons of your Father in heaven; for He makes His sun rise on the evil and on the good, and sends rain on the just and on the unjust. For if you love those who love you, what reward have you? Do not even the tax collectors do the same?" (Matt. 5:44–46)

"But love your enemies, do good, and lend, hoping for nothing in return; and your reward will be great, and you will be sons of the Most High. For He is kind to the unthankful and evil. Therefore, be merciful, just as your Father also is merciful." (Luke 6:35–36)

It may seem unusual that we should speak of God as "humble," though both St. Silouan and St. Sophrony speak quite strongly about this. It is the ground, we may say, of God's love. His love is impartial, not being used as a cudgel of reward and punishment. In His humility, God accepts us and encounters us as human to human in His Incarnation. And what we see in the Incarnation is the showing forth, the revelation of who God is. God did not become humble because He became a man. He became a man because He is humble.

That same humility is our path toward freedom from the tyranny of shame and envy. Fr. Zacharias Zacharou writes, "One of St. Silouan's teachings is this: that we need to find the 'deep heart,' and we find it only with humility, because pride buries the heart. Pride hinders love. Whoever is proud cannot love."[31]

The path toward such humility unavoidably requires our confrontation with shame. Contemporary psychology speaks of healing shame through growth in self-esteem. Strangely, the Tradition would describe this as growth in humility. Our

---

31 Archimandrite Zacharias Zacharou, *The Enlargement of the Heart* (Dalton, PA: Mt. Thabor Publishing, 2012), Kindle loc. 3286.

culture is rooted in individualism. In the secular world "self-esteem" is easily seen in isolation from everything around us. "I feel good about myself" is often mistaken for such self-esteem. Of course, not all self-esteem is healthy, particularly if it is rooted in a lie. To encourage someone to feel good about something that is, in fact, defective or lacking can be a nurturing in narcissism. Fr. Zacharias Zacharou offers an insightful definition of shame: "the lack of courage to see ourselves as God sees us." Healthy shame or humility, therefore, is having the "courage to see ourselves as God sees us," and thus, "seeing ourselves for who we are in truth." This could be understood as a proper and healthy self-esteem, if the Tradition were to use that term.

This humility, this healthy shame, requires the healing of the soul. The weaned child envisioned in the psalm is a healthy child whose sense of self is able to withstand various tests. Though childhood can be a place where such a foundation is established, other later experiences are able to damage the soul and create the conditions for shame—particularly for toxic shame. Something of the same process is required in the soul's healing at any stage of life. It is the assurance and constant reassurance of a mother's love that makes the soul of an infant stable in its foundation. (I do not mean to neglect the role of fathers in this process, but I see it in something of an auxiliary role in the earliest months of life.) Other persons will be required to fulfill this role later in life if the damage of whatever shame has occurred is to be healed. It is little wonder that the role of confessor in the early Celtic Church was described as that of a "soul friend" (*anam cara*).

If we are to love as God loves, including loving our enemies, then we must truly know that God loves us and how He loves us (as well as how He loves our enemies). That same love is required of the Christian community around us, including its spiritual leader. If there is damage to be healed, it should be understood that time is required. We were not likely damaged overnight, nor are we healed in that manner. In the meantime, the vulnerability and openness practiced in confession, met with the same vulnerability and openness of love—repeatedly, frequently, and consistently, together with teaching and the administration of the sacraments—works toward the transformation St. Paul describes: "But we all, with unveiled face, beholding as in a mirror the glory of the Lord, are being transformed into the same image from glory to glory, just as by the Spirit of the Lord" (2 Cor. 3:18).

It is important to recognize the culture of shame and envy that surrounds us and to practice a lifestyle that refuses to take part in it. If God causes His sun to shine on the just and the unjust, then we should offer our kindness and generosity to all, both friend and enemy. We are not in competition for the love of God or for the control of history. To declare ourselves as disciples of Christ is to declare that God alone is in charge of the outcome of history. The success of those who oppose us does not diminish us. Our souls should join with the psalmist and say, "O Israel, hope in the Lord from this time forth and forever more."

CHAPTER SEVEN

The Shame of Conversion

I HAVE BEEN A CONVERT MOST OF MY LIFE. I was born into a culturally Baptist family in South Carolina in the 1950s. At age ten, I left my family church and joined a different con-gregation (not much conversion involved at that point). At age thirteen, I dropped out of church (didn't convert, just didn't believe much). At age fifteen, I became an Episcopalian and got my first real taste of conversion (more later). At age seventeen, I became a Jesus freak and lived in a commune (conversion on steroids). At age twenty-one, I de-converted and went back to the Episcopalians (somewhat chagrined). At age forty-four, I became Eastern Orthodox (a conversion I'm still coming to understand). What I know for certain is that my story is not so unusual, even if it seems somewhat jumbled. Americans are converts. It's what we do.

Some years back, in a conversation with a Russian woman in my congregation, I was given some of my first insights into the American reality of conversion. I had baptized this woman and her entire family. They were unchurched Russians who had grown up in the Soviet Union. In the course of the conversation, I described her as a convert. She bristled in a manner I had never encountered. Her face was a demonstration of Russian disgust. "I am not a convert!" she protested. "I am Orthodox! [This she said in Russian.] I simply had never been baptized!" Then she added the full revelation: "Converts are people who *choose*!" I had never before heard the word *choose* used in a pejorative manner. In my head, however, I did the math. Americans are people who choose. It's what we do.

The dynamics of conversion have something of a double edge. There is a movement toward God, and there is a temptation toward the self. We tend to concentrate on the self when we choose; it's the shopper's temptation. What do we want in a converted self? Our culture has a long history of opportunities for conversion—religious movements with promises of instantaneous transformation. In 1859, Samuel Smiles published a book entitled *Self-Help*, cementing the phrase's place in our culture. The book's opening sentence, "God helps those who help themselves" (not a quote from Scripture), captured well the goal of many a conversion as well as the mechanisms too often employed.

To want to change, even *choose* to change, is not uncommon. Whether we are driven by inner pain or perceived outward appearances, shame is almost always a companion to our desires for transformation. The easiest transformations in our lives are those that go no deeper than outward identity. Leaving one club and joining another can serve as a quick fix for the self-as-identity. The hallmarks of identity—jargon, clothing, opinions, moral posturing—announce to the world (and to the false self) that we have become a new person. In that manner, the problems associated with a previous identity are quickly dispensed with and castigated as a mistake well enough abandoned.

A more difficult transformation is sought in our desire for inclusion. Conversion displaces us. Either we find ourselves displaced from somewhere we belonged before, or we find ourselves somewhere new, where our displacement has yet to be resolved. When I entered the Orthodox Church, it meant renouncing my ordination in the Episcopal Church. Thus I became a layman again. It was a loss of identity. No one told me I would experience it with shame. Indeed, even speaking of it in those terms felt like a betrayal of the conversion itself. Saint Paul, looking back at his time as a Pharisee prior to coming to Christ, wrote:

> If anyone else thinks he may have confidence in the flesh, I more so: circumcised the eighth day, of the stock of Israel, *of* the tribe of Benjamin, a Hebrew of the Hebrews; concerning the law, a Pharisee; concerning zeal, persecuting the church; concerning the righteousness which is in the law, blameless. (Phil. 3:4–6)

His Jewish pedigree was impeccable. Nonetheless, he added:

> But what things were gain to me, these I have counted loss for Christ. Indeed I also count all things loss for the excellence of the knowledge of Christ Jesus my Lord, for whom I have suffered the loss of all things, and count them as rubbish, that I may gain Christ and be found in Him, not

having my own righteousness, which *is* from the law, but that which *is* through faith in Christ, the righteousness which is from God by faith. (Phil 3:7–9)

It was a deep irony that Paul's arrest and trial came about through the instigation of his fellow Jews rather than from any persecution by the Gentiles. It was as though that part of his shame was made complete.

I recall that some journalist friends wanted to "do my story" shortly after my reception into the Orthodox Church. It would have been what has become a typical treatment: brave conservative leaves behind the growing problems within the Episcopal Church for a more traditional home. I refused the offer with a clear statement: "I have entered the Orthodox Church as a penitent, not as a beleaguered combatant. My story is for my confessor." At the same time, I quit writing and did not begin again for another eight years.

What I did not understand at the time was the shame I was experiencing. How can we feel shame over something we believe to have been right and good? As I understand it now, the shame came from the loss of identity—something that leaves an emptiness, even if the emptiness is preferable to the fullness you had before.

This is worth bearing in mind for the many converts who are entering the Church these days. The loss of identity need not rise to the level of a lost vocation or position. The lost familiarity of the past alone can be enough to trigger feelings of shame. Worse still, shame can easily go unidentified and thus unattended. We may also feel shame *because* we feel shame.

Saint Paul's response to his shame (though he does not name it as such) was to recognize the truth of what was taking place. In his Corinthian correspondence he rebuts the shame with a spate of boasting:

> Are they Hebrews? So *am* I. Are they Israelites? So *am* I. Are they the seed of Abraham? So *am* I. Are they ministers of Christ?—I speak as a fool—I *am* more: in labors more abundant, in stripes above measure, in prisons more frequently, in deaths often. From the Jews five times I received forty *stripes* minus one. Three times I was beaten with rods; once I was stoned; three times I was shipwrecked; a night and a day I have been in the deep; *in* journeys often, *in* perils of waters, *in* perils of robbers, *in* perils of *my own* countrymen, *in* perils of the Gentiles, *in* perils in the city, *in* perils in the wilderness, *in* perils in the sea, *in* perils among false brethren; in weariness and toil, in sleeplessness often, in hunger and thirst, in fastings often, in cold and nakedness. (2 Cor. 11:22–27)

His Philippian letter is traditionally held to be his last, written near the end of his life. There he no longer boasts of his accomplishments but only speaks of his longing to know Christ more fully. His words point toward the place where shame finds its final resolution, and the letter is instructive for thinking about that process.

If anything, Paul's Philippians passage describes a forgetting of self. "I count all things as loss for the excellence of the knowledge of Christ." He is not saying, "I'm willing to do whatever is necessary to be saved." He is quite specific about the content of what moves him forward: the knowledge of Christ. This is far deeper than any intellectual concept. He describes it as nothing less than a true participation in the life of Christ, both in His Resurrection and in His death—sharing in His sufferings: "that I may know Him and the power of His resurrection, and the communion of His sufferings, being conformed to His death" (Phil 3:10).

Saint Paul is reaching into the very depths of his soul, beholding the mirror itself. He goes beneath every element of his own shame and finds himself swallowed up in the image of Christ, suffering, crucified, and risen. The life of Christ has become his own life as well. In this manner, his own shame is not so much removed as it is resolved by becoming united with the life-giving shame of Christ. It has become healthy shame or humility. Earlier in the epistle, St. Paul urged his readers to have the "mind of Christ" within them, specifically the mind of Christ's "humility," His self-emptying (kenosis, Phil. 2:5–11).

Our own experience of shame is generally uncomfortable, something we flee. Saint Paul is not seeking this unpleasantness. He is no masochist or self-despising neurotic. Rather, as he describes it, he seeks the excellence of the knowledge of Christ.

Some years back, I did an interview with a YouTuber in which I was asked, "Why become Orthodox?" My answer came without hesitation: "Because you believe it to be the truth." I could think of no other reason. That said, there are any number of caveats that should follow.

If Orthodox Christianity is the truth, that does not mean it is "better" than other forms of Christianity. I'm not suggesting that Orthodoxy is worse or just the same. Rather, my point is that comparisons are a distraction for the most part, and they disguise subtle (and not so subtle) temptations for unresolved shame. Orthodoxy's unbroken history is a sad saga of sin and struggle that includes some of the most difficult times in the history of the Faith. When Orthodox Christianity makes a claim to be the truth, it is describing its historical continuity in faith, practice, and sacramental reality. I tell people that Orthodoxy is simply original, unimproved Christianity. American denominationalism tends to promote a consumerist approach to the Faith. In that world, we tend to look for elements to compare, with our own preferences largely serving as our guides.

Embracing Orthodox Christianity should mean stepping outside the consumer-based world of modernity. In some respects, the experience and reality of Orthodoxy will seem inferior to other things or loaded with unwanted baggage. It is a world fraught with ethnic stories and experiences that are foreign to the West. There are land mines that you would never expect. I have told people in jest that in becoming Orthodox, they should be prepared to be bored. Our services can be long and unfamiliar, especially at first. Nothing in our liturgical life evolved in a consumer context. Thus, as a matter of course, the services don't care whether you're bored or not. The modern concept of the congregation as an audience is alien to Orthodoxy. We gather to do the *work* of worship. Sometimes the work is hard. Interestingly, the word *liturgy* means "work of the people."

Shame can be involved in the displacement of what we have left behind. In the same manner, we may experience a shame that reflects the displacement of where we find ourselves when we arrive. As a result of these realities, it makes sense for priests to make themselves familiar with the dynamics of shame (particularly in its unexpected aspects) and the place it holds in a person's life. To welcome a convert is to invite her into her own shame as well as the collective shame of the Church. Such a statement runs deeply counter to the pleasure-centered culture in which we dwell, to say nothing of a culture that avoids shame whenever possible. Being up front about this aspect of a convert's struggle can help him negotiate the disappointments that inevitably arise.

The fullness of the Orthodox Tradition contains a deep and living memory of the very depths of human experience, particularly as that experience is plunged into the depths of union with Christ. When St. Paul expresses a desire for communion in the sufferings of Christ, there is nothing morbid at work. He could just as easily have called for communion with the *love* of Christ. However, such an expression would be grossly distorted in a culture that romanticizes love and often reduces it to mere sentimentality. Who doesn't want love? But the love that is made known to us in Christ is a revelation of the inner life of God. It is the Father pouring Himself into the Son as the Son empties Himself into the Father. It is the Holy Spirit who speaks nothing of Himself but only of the Son (John 16:13). This mutual divine humility is the fullest expression of love. It is life given as gift, received as gift, and offered again as gift. Thus, we can describe two essential actions within that life as it has been passed down to us by Tradition: self-emptying and thanksgiving. Both are actions that express the reality of humility.

I recall a young man who told me of his own conversion to Orthodoxy. He had attended a church for over six months and had been engaged in numerous conversations with the priest. As time went on, he noticed that the priest never asked him if he wanted to convert. Somewhat puzzled, he broached the subject himself. The priest said he was waiting to be asked. The young man told me he was struck by the fact that the priest "never tried to close the sale." His previous experience in churches had always been as the recipient of a sales pitch. At the time, I was struck by the wisdom of his priest.

The modern spirit of consumerism nurtures and feeds our tendencies towards tribalism, or the use of identity as a shield against shame. In this context, Orthodoxy can easily become a mere brand of Christianity. Of course, Orthodoxy is not a *brand*. It was the form of Christianity when there was no other. Orthodoxy is diminished, I think, when it becomes one brand among many. We must acknowledge that it is often impossible for Orthodoxy to speak in its authentic voice when confronted by other Christian formulations. In the Nicene Creed we confess that the Church is "One, Holy, Catholic, and Apostolic." It cannot come in "twos." The modern suggestion is that we should say all churches are, in reality, "one church," but this is a betrayal of the Creed and the true nature of the Church. The difficulty in expressing this comes from the simple fact that Orthodoxy has no language to describe denominational Christianity. It could be called "schismatic," though that is something of an anachronism.

This difficulty in speaking to our present landscape can itself be a source of shame. When family members or friends who are not Orthodox discover that they cannot receive communion, for example, or that Orthodoxy describes itself as the "One" Church, their dismay can leave a convert exposed, accused of an animosity that is not real. This is a common experience among converts to Orthodoxy. I have known more than a few who delayed their reception into the Church for fear of offending those who would feel left behind. Oddly, what they are expressing is their own shame—something that will likely never be described by that name, nor can it be resolved in a healthy manner until it is. It is important to understand, however, that the shame provoked by conversion is not a bad thing. Shame is a signal, not a punishment or necessarily a result of wrongdoing.

Conversion, of course, is something that belongs to all Orthodox believers, despite the protestations of those who were born into an Orthodox culture or family. No matter how pure the pedigree, every one of us has a journey to make toward union with Christ and the uncovering of the true self. Such a journey never comes as a birthright but only in the course of a lifetime of conversion—which is another word for repentance and transformation.

It has become a commonplace in recent years to speak about the impact of converts on American Orthodoxy. For some, the influx of converts has become a convenient scapegoat for whatever troubles them about the Church. Sometimes, I myself am troubled about our converts and have to remind myself that I am one of them. No doubt, convert culture is not the same as the more settled ethnic cultures that receive the converts. A half century back, it would likely have been impossible to find young men excitedly discussing theories of the atonement at coffee hour. Some may rightly think, "This is not my grand-father's Orthodoxy." On the other hand, the last century may have seen ethnic parishioners locked in bitter dispute about various European issues that would have been alien to main-stream American culture—although American religion (Prot-estantism in particular) has always been deeply enmeshed in political thought.[32]

It would be a rare thing indeed to see people shed their cul-ture when they come into the Church. For better or for worse, the movement of converts into American Orthodoxy is per-haps the first true engagement of Orthodoxy with America itself. It behooves us to remember this as well as to under-stand that this engagement is in its infancy. We will inevitably get it wrong as we move toward discovering what it means to get it right.

The negative reactions to convert Orthodoxy that are voiced from time to time are themselves a product of shame, or at least not a sentiment devoid of shame. The first great struggle with shame of any sort is to recognize it for what it is and to call it by its true name. The second great struggle is to bring it into the presence of Christ and sit with it, seeking neither to distance ourselves, to blame others, nor to avoid His gaze.

---

32 The religious movements of seventeenth-century England, which were highly political at the time, were transplanted to America in its colonial period. As religious movements and revivals have formed and shaped Protestant churches through time, so have they formed and shaped American culture and politics. The "Whig" movement in politics, which gave rise to what would become both populist and liberal politics, was an outgrowth of early evangelical religious movements. Without them, there would have been no abolitionists, no prohibitionists, no feminism, etc. It is not inaccurate to describe America the *political* experiment as America the *religious* experiment.

I have increasingly come to understand Orthodox Christianity for what it is—not the ideal Church, much less the perfect Church. It is not a bulwark against an alien and hostile culture. It is not the Church that got everything right while everyone else got it wrong. It is, I believe, *the* Church. To say that is to acknowledge that it is the meeting point where God is gathering all things together in one, in Christ Jesus. Such a meeting point is inevitably messy because of the nature of who we ourselves are. We cannot see Christ face to face without, at the same time, encountering our own shame. And in the context of the Church, we encounter not just our own shame, but that of the whole world. This is Christ crucified.

CHAPTER EIGHT

The Shame of Male and Female

My soul shall rejoice in the Lord, for He has clothed Me with
the garment of salvation; He has covered me with the robe of
gladness; as a bridegroom He has set a crown on me; and as
a bride adorns herself with jewels, so has He adorned me.
—ISAIAH 61:10, QUOTED IN
THE VESTING PRAYERS IN THE LITURGY

I HAVE PRESIDED AT COUNTLESS WEDDINGS in my years as a priest. I have never seen a bride I thought was less than radiant. At the same time, I suspect many of the brides worried that their appearance was less than or other than what they desired. What most imagine for that day is something transcendent, a beauty that may have been the object of the imagination for years, perhaps beginning in the mind of a little girl. Powerful symbols and archetypes inform every wedding, as though we were caught up in a grand drama of salvation.

That much of this is unconscious and revolves around the dynamics of shame—our most unconscious emotion—is not surprising. It is also nearly universal. Almost every culture surrounds the event of a wedding with powerful symbols, often marked with special garments. Even in the deeply secularized atheism of the Soviet regime, when churches were closed, precluding the drama of traditional Russian weddings, many churches were converted into "wedding palaces," places where some of the pageantry of the past could be reenacted without the baggage of Christian belief. Wedding magic is written deep in our psyche.

We can learn a great deal from watching children. As much as we might imagine them as the products of their culture (which, to some extent, they always are), they are also examples of things that are writ large in the soul and psyche of us all. That children learn by playing games (see Jean Piaget's theory of cognitive development) should be obvious. They not only copy adults; they reenact our lives. Among the many games children enjoy are versions of dress-up. I cannot recount how many times young "princesses" have appeared at the chalice in church of a Sunday, complete with tiara and the occasional tutu. Of course, I have my own crown (if one can so describe a *kamilavka*—a priest's hat), awarded me by my bishop. What I know for certain is that the game of dressing up rhymes with the serious business of vesting a priest, and that both reveal something important about who we are and the nature of our human existence.

We all have an intuition attached to robes of beauty and wonder. It is far more than putting on adult clothes or mimicking a scene in a movie. I am profoundly convinced that the movies are secondary. We were dreaming of such robes long before we ever saw them on a screen or in a book. What we see on a screen resonates because it acts as a mirror for something that has dwelt within us through the ages. We want *what the robes promise to give us*—and what they promise is ever so much more than being a king or queen.

What is at work on a number of levels is the dynamic of shame and nakedness. That dynamic, if considered only on the level of *literal* nakedness, is insufficient to account for the mythic and symbolic power of the robing. Our literal nakedness reflects something far more profound, far more cosmic. The story of the nakedness of Adam and Eve continues to have power and meaning, regardless of how one views the actual text of Scripture. Indeed, those who treat the Scriptures in an extremely literal manner run the risk of overlooking the greater power within the story. For Adam and Eve are not just the first human beings in the story; they are all human beings throughout all time. The Fall is repeated, relived, in numberless ways through the ages, and even numberless times within each single life. The rupture of communion with God is also a rupture of communion with ourselves and all creation around us. It is particularly a rupture of communion with other human beings, and intensely a rupture of communion that intrudes into the relationship of marriage. Genesis 3 introduces the notion of marriage or marital union between male and female, as well as that of child-bearing, but it describes it under the rubrics or shadow of brokenness.

To the woman He said: "I will greatly multiply your sorrow and your conception; in pain you shall bring forth children; your desire *shall be* for your husband, and he shall rule over you."

Then to Adam He said, "Because you have heeded the voice of your wife, and have eaten from the tree of which I commanded you, saying, 'You shall not eat of it': Cursed is the ground for your sake; In toil you shall eat of it all the days of your life. Both thorns and thistles it shall bring forth for you, and you shall eat the herb of the field. In the sweat of your face you shall eat bread till you return to the ground, For out of it you were taken; For dust you are, and to dust you shall return." (Gen. 3:16–19)

St. Ephrem of Syria pictured Adam in a priestly role, the Garden of Paradise set on the pinnacle of a mountain serving as the temple of God. However, Adam fails in his task and disobeys the commandment of God. His nakedness is not just a revelation of his physical state but the revelation that he has lost his priestly robe—an image of our right and full communion with God and thus with all things.

> God did not permit
> Adam to enter
> that innermost tabernacle;
> this was withheld,
> so that first he might prove pleasing
> in his service to that outer Tabernacle;
> like a priest
> with fragrant incense,
> Adam's keeping of the commandment

was to be his censer;
that he might enter before the Hidden One
into that Hidden Tabernacle.[33]
(*Hymns of Paradise* III.16)

There is, hidden within the heart of us all, a deep yearning for that original state, a place where all things are rightly ordered, where our communion with God shines as an enfolding robe of glory. That robing echoes a crowning moment when, standing before God, one might hear, "Well done, good and faithful servant."

Of course, human experience is rarely couched in such theological terms. Often we have no name for our deepest longings, or we call them by names that have been substituted—only to discover to our own chagrin that the substitute wasn't quite the thing we wanted. The fantasy that is fulfilled in many modern weddings is likely just such a thing. The pageantry can be magnificent and expensive. The dress is the most obvious star of the modern wedding. Its white color was originally associated with purity and virginity, which in our modern context is assumed to be a thing of the past, a quaint notion regarding human sexuality. However, the dress itself does not lie: it is just such innocence and purity that we seek and hunger for, the possibility of communion that carries no element of shame. On that day, the wearer of the dress is the object of admiration, a symbol of perfection and wonder. Though it lasts less than an hour in modern ceremonies, neither its anticipation nor its memory is limited by time.

---

33 *Hymns on Paradise*, trans. Sebastian Brock (Crestwood, NY: St. Vladimir's Seminary Press, 1990), 96.

Grooms play a subsidiary role, with the exception that the symbol of perfection and wonder is awarded to them as their own. Orthodox weddings have added features, unknown to the West, that augment the somewhat meager imagery in Western traditions. It has always interested me that there are no vows included in an Orthodox wedding. They have a way of marring the magic in Western ceremonies.

> (*Name*), wilt thou have this man/woman to be thy wedded husband/wife to live together after God's ordinance in the Holy Estate of matrimony? Wilt thou love him/her, comfort him/her, honor and keep him/her, in sickness and in health, and forsaking all others keep thee only unto him/her as long as you both shall live?" ("I will")

With this promise of a sort of moral perfection, there are (off stage, as it were) clouds of doubt. Will we in fact do these things? The ceremony is easily haunted by echoes of our many failures.

In an Orthodox wedding, the ceremony is unmarred by such suggestions. Whatever struggles a couple might endure, they are crowned as martyrs, thus sanctifying even the failures that may come their way. The bride may well be clothed in white, but the center of the day is found in the crowns (indeed, in many Orthodox languages, weddings are called "crownings"). In the Oriental Orthodox tradition, couples are not only crowned on their wedding day but robed as well. This is in full keeping with Orthodox understanding.

It is not in the least accidental that there is a great similarity between the Orthodox service for the ordination of a priest and an Orthodox wedding. Just as the wedding couple is led three times around a central table in the church, so a priest is led three times around the altar. And lest we miss the intended similarity, the same three hymns (troparia) are sung. Indeed, some go so far as to say that a priest is "being married to the altar." A highlight in the ordination comes at the vesting of the priest. As each item of his vestments is placed on him, the bishop pauses, looks to the congregation and intones, "Axios!" ("He is worthy!") The people respond, "Axios! Axios! Axios!" In many ways, it is like a wedding on steroids.

If a bride stands in the symbolic (or literal) place of a virgin, affirmed in her white dress, unmarked by shame, the newly ordained priest stands in a similar place of affirmation, gloriously appareled, with onlookers shouting repeatedly that he is "worthy." Of course, the priest knows that he is not worthy, that he is being vested for and placed in a position to which he is inadequate. As the years go by, he will become ever more aware that the moment of his ordination was a momentary echo of something greater, something eschatological, which he can only long for and pray that it will someday be fulfilled. For our lives, both those of brides and those of priests, are marked by shame, by a naked truth that would betray any pretense of innocence or worthiness.

We long to be clothed (as St. Paul says in 2 Cor. 5:2), and this is on the deepest level of our psyche. Kings or their equivalents are robed and crowned across a wide variety of cultures, just as priests and shamans are noted by their clothing, or a bride is adorned in her wedding finery. In all of these cases and many similar ones, the clothing serves not only to cover up the quotidian blandness of our personas, but also to suggest that the glorious dream of an exaltation beyond shame is possible—somewhere, somehow. We dream of it.

It is deeply fitting that the mystery of our being robed in the presence of others should take place in the context of a wedding. For in the marriage that begins on that day, a fearful disrobing will ensue, accompanied by a potential for shame that far transcends our naked bodies. The awkwardness of sex (often the object of comedy) only serves to reflect the deeper awkwardness of our naked souls. The sexual revolution and the ubiquity of porn have served to create an imaginary world of universal sexual prowess and mastery. But what we imagine only serves to mock us, and even destroy us, in the real world that is the dance of human sexual interaction. Just as the bedroom is connected to the rest of the house, so our sex lives come burdened with every word spoken earlier in the day or week. Every broken promise, every wounding word or glance, every failure of love and kindness enters into this most intimate of spaces. No doubt, we may perform a psychological dance in which we seek to block out unwanted thoughts and live a compartmentalized existence, but such strategies are seldom successful. Children, careers, and a myriad of other distractions may fill the gaps for many. But such distractions are a far cry from the promise represented in the glorious clothing of a shame-free moment.

More than all other things, it is shame that dogs our relationships and hardens our hearts. Disappointed expectations, unwanted exposure, exclusion—all classical triggers for shame, each of which has its own vocabulary and synonymous emotions—dot the path of marriage as surely as we live and breathe. We are frequently ill-equipped to name our emotions, particularly those that are embedded in shame. To speak their names is to reinvite the shame itself. It is little wonder that shame most often morphs into either anger or sadness. However, anger and sadness do not resolve shame. They serve only to mask it and to leave it unattended and unhealed. As a result, the glorious wonder of a wedding day (or other such moments) is traded in for a suit of armor that encloses the heart. As a result, we do not know ourselves, for it is only in the heart that the secret of our being can be known. By the same token, we struggle to know God, for He is wrapped in the same secret that guards the heart. The only path forward, toward ourselves and toward God—as well as the only path toward the healing of marriages, ministries, and other relationships—is through shame itself.

Sexual intimacy is only the most profound of the many intimacies that make up our lives. That we frequently get it wrong should come as no surprise. We really do not know what we're doing and mistake the physical mechanics of desire and satisfaction for the point of the exercise. In fact, the physical is only the most obvious part of the activity; what is unspoken and unseen is by far the larger and more important part. For all of human history that we know, cultures have surrounded both the context and content of sexual intimacy with rules. Who participates, what takes place, and so much more of the context seek to preserve some measure of safety and predictability.

The sexual revolution (which many date to the 1960s) is only one of modernity's efforts to deny some of the most natural, or least artificial, aspects of human life. The technologies surrounding birth control have, among many other things, allowed the creation of alternative narratives regarding our sexual lives as well as alternative ways of describing the whole of human history. The most obvious thing about sex is its place within the process of procreation. Most of the mores and rules that have surrounded sex through the ages have, in one manner or another, served a role as protector of the consequences of sexual activity and the familial responsibilities required. We may imagine that God made sex pleasurable in order to encourage us to procreate. But in a pleasure-seeking society, this fact leads people to attempt to divorce sex from procreation entirely. Contemporary culture has sought to treat sex as an end in itself, driven primarily by lifestyle and our desire for personal pleasure.

No matter how sex is reframed in a culture, it remains a fundamental, physical fact of life that no amount of storytelling can actually change. Equally fundamental is the experience of shame that is embedded within it. Every attempt to alter the narrative, to create a shame-free sexual experience, only tinkers around the edges of something that will not be tamed or forced into ideologically imagined frameworks.

The traditional framework associated with Christian teaching about sex has been a convenient target for many, with the contention that it has created a shame-bound world of homophobia, transphobia, and so forth. Of course, the Christian teaching that is being assaulted is a caricatured product of the arguer's imagination. The truth is that the Christian teaching transcends human sexual experience and speaks with awe and wonder about a mystery that reaches even into salvation itself. Christian proscriptions are little more than tiny warning labels on a very large bomb, speaking mostly about taking care with something that is dangerous and easily exploded. It is of note that the union of husband and wife is cited in Scripture as the most apt analogy of the relationship between God and His Church. This is nearly tantamount to saying that it is symbolic of everything in human existence.

As deeply personal as is the intimacy of marriage, it remains an encounter with things that are timeless, an embodiment of the greatest drama in all history. And yet, we experience the shame that surrounds it in small and poignant ways. Marriage is a dance. We reveal ourselves and hide ourselves. Its promise is so utterly profound that it can hardly be overestimated, but the reality generally falls short, in lesser ways or greater. The measure of love and safety required to reveal the fullness of our naked self is beyond our reach. It requires more than another human being can give. It requires the grace of God.

Humility as an Erotic Necessity

C. S. LEWIS HAD INTERESTING insights into the relationship of male and female, particularly for a man who was unmarried until late in his life, and even then married under unusual circumstances. Nonetheless, he wrote profoundly about love and taught authoritatively about the notion of courtly love as found in the Middle Ages, something about which he may be regarded as one of the world's greatest authorities. There was to an extent a true of sense of platonic love in that strange period of Western history. That is to say, there was a recognition that human beings were not so much the creators of their own realities as they were participants in a larger Reality that formed and shaped everything that mattered in this world. Every small love was a reflection of a greater love and took its significance from that fact.

In his novel *That Hideous Strength*, Lewis applied this understanding to a young couple, Mark and Jane Studdock. While cosmic forces are locked in a battle for the future of the earth, so Mark and Jane are living out a personal struggle that is not unrelated to the cosmic. The two are both struggling with career-related concerns that are devouring their marriage. Mark has accepted a university position, but his own way forward is marked with shame (largely experienced as being "on the outside") that leads him into a dangerous position. Jane struggles with her marriage, feeling cut off from earlier career concerns, lonely, and isolated as Mark focuses on his own worries. Their marriage is a subplot of this supernatural novel that may, in fact, be the main plot.

In a crucial conversation, Jane confronts a conflict between equality and the notion of obedience. She has always championed the former and is staggered by the suggestion that obedience should play any role in a modern relationship. She is told, "It is not your fault. They never warned you. No one has ever told you that obedience—humility—is an erotic necessity. You are putting equality just where it ought not to be."

Additionally she hears, "you do not fail in obedience through lack of love, but have lost love because you never attempted obedience."[34] To her mind, obedience and humility are threats to

_____

34 C. S. Lewis, *That Hideous Strength* (New York: Scribner, 1996), 145–46.

equality, and without equality, she feels she risks losing herself and everything she has worked for. Lewis is intentionally challenging certain modern notions of human relations.

It is no use trying to make the inner life of the heart conform to economic and political notions of reality. The heart is not a law court, nor is the Constitution a map to the human soul. Efforts to redefine and reimagine human sexuality tend to run into an intransigent reality that cannot be blamed on Christianity or hatred or some human perversity. Some argue that the imagery in our inherited stories and myths is the product of culture. There is, I think, a stronger case to be made that culture (along with its inherited stories and myths) is the product of something far older than humanity itself. That much of our life rhymes with the animal kingdom is no mistake or accident. The animals are a product of the same eternal verities as human beings. We are actors in a drama that was ancient before the world came into existence.

The spiritual journey is not an exercise in modern psychology or a path to becoming "well-adjusted." It is a journey through difficult places within the heart toward a Reality that is formed and shaped by God. It is not a product of culture or ideology. The primary orientation toward such things, like our primary orientation toward each other, is properly one of humility. It is as if we faced a huge mountain with the object of getting to the other side. If our strategy were to bore a tunnel through the mountain or to blow the mountain into tiny bits, that would be an arrogance of massive proportions. It is more proper to acknowledge the reality of the mountain and to learn to climb.

In the same manner, the reality of male and female confronts each of us with a mountain of unchangeable reality. Indeed, to a great extent, those with whom we are in relation do not fully understand their own selves. We are always mutually subject to our own shame and must mutually find our way over the various mountains that it presents.

We never know or understand what we are getting ourselves into when we marry. This is generally the case in all relationships but particularly so in marriage. No other relationship has at its core the encounter with intimacy over such an extended time as marriage brings. Of no other do we say, "This is bone of my bone and flesh of my flesh." Ideally, in marriage we see in the other a revelation of our own self. Ideally, it comes to be that we know ourselves only as we see ourselves in the beloved. Everything that clothes the self in falseness, therefore, renders the self opaque and inhibits the fulfillment of the marriage bond.

The bearing of shame (and thus, the virtue of humility) generally requires safety and the knowledge that the vulnerability that is shared will not later be weaponized or shared with others to whom it was not given. Marriage introduces us to a life of "giftedness," in which each spouse offers to the other the unique gift of his or her self. In my experience, this gift becomes even greater with the blessing of children (should a couple be so blessed). A child is a literal fulfillment of the marriage union, "bone of bone" and "flesh of flesh." Children also have a profound way of mirroring parents, both for good and for ill. We easily see ourselves in them—something that can often provoke shame in unexpected ways.

The bearing of shame within the context of marriage is strangely similar to worship, though very few today would understand such a statement. In the marriage ceremony in the earliest English *Book of Common Prayer* (1552), as the groom places a ring on the bride's finger, he says, "With this ring I thee wed: with my body I thee worship: and with all my worldly goods I thee endow."

The phrase "with my body I thee worship" easily scandalizes listeners, who immediately assume it must mean something other than what it says. Indeed, "worship" in this older sense could easily be translated "venerate." It is a distinction the Orthodox understand full well. Worship, as we use the word today, belongs to God alone, but we venerate icons, the relics of saints, and other things and persons that are worthy of such honor. The trouble is that, in the minds of many moderns, both worship and veneration have come to mean so much less than was once intended.

Worship from the heart requires both awe and wonder, neither of which is possible without healthy shame. Perhaps the most essential act of worship directed toward God is that of thanksgiving, offering to God the recognition that all we have and all we are comes from Him. It is an act of humility in which we acknowledge ourselves as the recipients of gifts and, more particularly, the recipients of His goodness. However, in a democratically conceived world (as we imagine ourselves to be "equals"), we frequently have a hard time extending such veneration toward another human being. Nonetheless, awe and wonder are necessities for love.

The lively debates surrounding human sexuality that have marked the past fifty years or more do not, I think, represent a great and lasting change in human culture. If anything, the noise and tension created by their assertions are greater now than at any time in the past. In many ways, the failure of our time lies in our truncated vision of what it means to be human. Equality is an insufficient way to speak about who we are. Nor is it true that we ever behave as neutered individuals. Maleness and femaleness are fundamental facts of our existence.

The Genesis account suggests that this distinction has been problematic since the beginning. To stand before one another naked and angry is no solution at all. Only love solves anything, and love requires not equality but humility, the ability to hold the other in wonder and to receive him or her as gift. No book (or chapter in a book) can reliably describe how men and women should be together. One man is not all men, and one woman is not all women. It can be said, however, that awe and wonder make love possible, marked as they are by humility—the ability to bear the burden of shame in the presence of another (and of oneself). Experience says this is a very slow process. That is one reason that marriages are intended to last for a lifetime.

Shame denies the wonder of who we are, as well as the wonder we feel for others. The modern anxiety that seeks to assert the self against all comers places shame as the hidden master of our lives, mistrusting the giftedness of our existence. The laws of our culture and our internalization of their fabrications presume a world of competition and violence. It is an occasion of deep sadness for me when a couple comes for counseling and begins to recite each other's failures to live up to demands and expectations. Often, they look for a priest to correct a wayward party, to act as a spiritual lawyer, perhaps giving rules that will make things right. The sickness, however, is not in the rules but in the soul. There is no law that can encompass wonder or behold the pure giftedness of another human life. Laws seek to set boundaries on shame, but they do so by invoking shame. They always fail to repair love. The wonder that welcomes the gift that is before us, however, stands free in its humility, not bound by shame nor denying it. It is an empty vessel that waits to be filled, the embodiment of love.

It is of paramount significance that St. Paul describes the relationship between Christ and His Church, and thus that between God and humanity, as being imaged in the relationship of husband and wife. We hold it to be essential in our understanding that human beings are created in the image and likeness of God. We often forget the full text of that verse of Scripture:

So God created man in his *own* image,
in the image of God he created him;
male and female he created them. (Gen. 1:27)

The mystery of the *imago Dei* is to be found in the mystery of male and female and, as St. Paul notes, particularly in the mystery of husband and wife (Eph. 5:32). This relational union, which so often frustrates our efforts when it fails, is also the primary icon of what it means to be human, created in the image and likeness of God. It is a relationship of intimacy that, to flourish, requires us to relinquish our efforts to hide. As such, it is the most emotionally dangerous relationship we can enter. This kind of vulnerability can only be offered as a gift, never forced or coerced. But inasmuch as we progress in intimacy, so it also represents the potential for true discovery, to know the self beyond and beneath the many veils of shame that darken the soul. This is only possible in a mutual sharing of protection and safety in which the well-being and inner prosperity of the one is sought in the well-being and inner prosperity of the other. In marriage, the lover knows himself in the soul of the other. We become mirrors of one another, a reflection made possible in love.

This same reality, we must remember, is a reflection of what exists between Christ and His Church. Christ is the Bridegroom of the soul, just as the soul is the bride of Christ.[35] This mystical marriage embodies the whole of the spiritual life, one in which we are always seeking the truth of who we are as revealed in the face of Christ. In His face, it is not shame that we encounter, an effort to push us away. Rather, it is the face of Him who ever seeks His bride that she might be presented "without spot or blemish" (Eph. 5:27). It is the great love story of the ages.

---

35 We can equally say that Christ is the Bridegroom of the Church, just as the Church is the bride of Christ. What is true of the Church is true of the soul.

CHAPTER NINE

The Shame of Gratitude

Among the more prominent goals of our culture is that of living well, with minimal pain and maximum prosperity (happiness). Who doesn't want to be happy? If you are among those who think of themselves as "moral," those goals will include some measure of doing good for others.

It is in this sort of context that many modern treatments of shame take shape. Shame is often treated as a problem or an affliction, and those suffering from shame are described as victims. This treatment, while well-intended, tends to obscure the place of normative, healthy shame in the human life. It isolates the tragic, toxic forms of shame and makes of them the whole of the story. Shame in its healthy form is an unavoidable and necessary part of our daily lives. Most people have little understanding of healthy shame, and our culture lacks the vocabulary to converse effectively about it. If the work in this book is of any use, I pray particularly that it will give readers a better understanding of the nature of our inner life and the dynamics that give us the most difficulties. This chapter will focus particularly on practices that allow healthy shame—distinguished from toxic forms—to be a useful part of our lives, anchored in a Tradition of wisdom that restores it to its proper place. The cornerstones of that practice are humility and gratitude. There is more to both of these than meets the eye.

There will never be a time in this life when shame is not present. This is not a theological statement or an idea rooted in a notion of our moral deserts. The simple reason for this is that shame in its healthy form is not a problem or a failure. It is not a symptom of something gone wrong. Healthy shame is a symptom of *normalcy*. It has a key role to play in our lives, a role that is complicated by the frequent distortions brought about by toxic situations and injuries.

Shame has been described as the "master emotion" in that it plays a key role in regulating the expression of our other emotions and our awareness of them. Often we experience a certain awkwardness around emotions. We're not certain whether we should share them with others. Indeed, we are often uncomfortable with the simple fact of *having* emotions. Shame is at the core of how we interact with others. When we are in a conversation, we often feel our way forward, particularly if the conversation is important or sensitive. The emotion that guides that feeling consists largely of the signals sent to us by the shame affect. It warns us and guides us. Those who lack this as a skill often find difficult conversations nearly impossible. As much as possible, they simply avoid them.

Scripture and the spiritual Tradition of the Church are no strangers to shame. They recognize its presence and offer guidance for how it is to be approached. They teach us how to heal shame when it has become a toxic burden, but more importantly, they point toward a way of living with it in its healthy form.

Scripture alone would likely be insufficient to offer this guidance. It is a large body of writings whose composition spans some thousand years or more. It is not systematic. Those who engage in scriptural interpretation as though the Bible were self-interpreting ("the Bible says") are either being disingenuous or are simply unaware of how their own hidden assumptions are guiding that process. In Orthodoxy, the approach to Scripture is to read it through the experience of the saints. In this manner, we ask not only "What does this mean?" but also, "What does this meaning look like when it is lived?" Even greater than these touchstones is the example of Christ Himself. In the case of the saints, we are seeing nothing more than lives that have sought to walk in union with Christ. Saint John wrote, "No one has seen God at any time. The only begotten Son, who is in the bosom of the Father, He has declared [interpreted] *Him*" (John 1:18).

Saint Paul gathers the gospel into a single image and directs the faithful toward its imitation:

Let this mind be in you which was also in Christ Jesus, who, being in the form of God, did not consider it robbery to be equal with God, but made Himself of no reputation, taking the form of a bondservant, *and* coming in the likeness of men. And being found in appearance as a man, He humbled Himself and became obedient to *the point of* death, even the death of the cross. Therefore, God also has highly exalted Him and given Him the name which is above every name, that at the name of Jesus every knee should bow, of those in heaven, and of those on earth, and of those under the earth, and *that* every tongue should confess that Jesus Christ *is* Lord, to the glory of God the Father. (Phil. 2:5–11)

It would have been possible for St. Paul to choose some other moment in the life and ministry of Christ as the mark of the Christian mind. He could have singled out an instance of forgiveness or generosity. He could have focused on an occasion of righteous indignation (which would likely have been very popular). Instead, he zeroes in on the Cross and the extreme humility Christ displayed in that moment. Indeed, the humility is so extreme that St. Paul describes it as "emptying Himself" (translated here as "humbled Himself"). One simple explanation of this admonition is that humility is the key to all the virtues.[36]

An Athonite elder is quoted as saying, "Humility acts like a magnet, drawing to it the grace of God."[37] This follows the Scripture: "Surely He scorns the scornful, / But gives grace to the humble" (Prov. 3:34). This is not a magical formula. It is a description of how we work. If shame is the master emotion, the gatekeeper, for the operation of our whole emotional life, then the ability to bear healthy shame in a healthy manner allows the whole of our inner life to move forward without the reactive interference that finds shame unbearable. This description sounds rather cold and

---

36 A saying attributed to St. Anthimos of Chios goes, "Humility will bring all the virtues." The same thought is found in the common Orthodox saying that humility is the "queen of the virtues." See Thomas Hopko, *Orthodox Spirituality* (Yonkers, NY: Department of Religious Education, Orthodox Church in America, 1981). Kindle Edition, loc. 966.
37 From the *Athonite Gerontikon*.

clinical, far less poetic than saying "humility will bring all the virtues." But I think it is important to be able to focus clearly on the mechanics of what is taking place.

Saint Paul was writing not so much to generations of Christians to come as to a church in Philippi. The Church is a community of grace, strangers gathered from various elements of society who are then asked to become a community that incarnates the love of God for the sake of the whole world. Paul's letters are filled with practical advice, efforts to instruct us in the life of heaven, paradise on earth. Writing to the Corinthians, he soared into poetic ecstasy as he described the nature of love:

> Love suffers long *and* is kind; love does not envy; love does not parade itself, is not puffed up; does not behave rudely, does not seek its own, is not provoked, thinks no evil; does not rejoice in iniquity, but rejoices in the truth; bears all things, believes all things, hopes all things, endures all things. (1 Cor. 13:4–7)

When love fails to suffer long and be kind, when it falls into envy—in short, when love fails to be love—it is most likely the case that it has fallen victim to shame. Unable to bear that burden, it reacts with envy, blame, and judgment, and makes every effort to protect a wounded self and to attack in return.

Saint Paul was not a Stoic. He was not writing to give instructions in living a well-ordered emotional life. What he describes is nothing less than the life of grace. The crucified Christ and His humility on the Cross are not exhibited as moral examples—"He was good, so you be good." Rather, St. Paul begins his exhortation with a fundamental assertion and reminder: "Let this mind be in you which was also in Christ Jesus." This "mind" is nothing other than Christ Himself. Our co-crucifixion with Christ is not something that occurs in imitation—it is His actual crucifixion united to us, making His life to be our life. "I have been crucified with Christ; it is no longer I who live, but Christ lives in me; and the *life* which I now live in the flesh I live by faith in the Son of God, who loved me and gave Himself for me" (Gal. 2:20).

A very specific instance of that crucifixion is manifest in our humility, as we patiently endure the trial of healthy shame in order to live in union with Christ and in love with others. The Catholic Saint Thérèse of Lisieux wondrously said, "If you can bear serenely the trial of being displeasing to yourself, then you will be for Jesus a pleasant place of shelter."[38]

The English philosopher Thomas Hobbes described the world in terms of constantly warring powers. "The state of nature is a state of war" is a succinct summary of his thought. He went on to describe our social life as a series of negotiated contracts in which we agree to cooperate for our own private advantage. His philosophy has provided more than a few political thinkers with their view of the world. Unfortunately, it accurately describes the human community more often than not. If we were to focus on the dynamic of shame and its role as the master emotion, we could describe the human community as individuals bound by shame as they encounter one another,

---

38 *Collected Letters of St. Thérèse of Lisieux*, trans. F. J. Sheed (London: Sheed and Ward, 1949), 265.

locked in a constant dance in which each seeks to avoid shame and its discomfort while making demands on others.

Sadly, this vision of the human community is sometimes lived out in a parish. We describe such relationships as walking on eggshells or avoiding land mines. If shame is unaddressed and humility is absent, human interaction becomes emotionally dangerous. At its worst, it becomes a colony of hell. It is in the setting of such broken communities that we must read St. Paul. It is one of the reasons his advice remains so timeless. The path of humility, in union with the self-emptying Crucifixion of Christ, is the single path to sanity in a shame-bound world. The joy that is found in intimacy and the bond of love lies just beyond the gates of humility. It is an earthly paradise.

As important as the practice of humility may be, it has the weakness of being passive. We cannot "do" humility as a thing in itself—it is practiced in response to something. My experience over the years has consistently shown the weakness of doing a negative. When we battle a bad habit, for example, simply not doing it is seldom effective. Something good must be done in its place. Life is best lived in the active voice. Not surprisingly, there is an active voice in the practice of humility. *The giving of thanks is humility in the active voice.*

It is possible to dismiss the giving of thanks as being among the most prosaic of human activities. It is an inherent part of polite behavior as we dance in the give-and-take of kindness or mere niceness. It is also the most profound of human actions, being largely synonymous with the action of worship. On the one hand, giving thanks can seem an empty gesture. On the other hand, it can be the most sublime of all expressions in which the words and actions of thanksgiving are accompanied by the offering of the whole self.

Saint Paul wrote, "I beseech you therefore, brethren, by the mercies of God, that you present your bodies a living sacrifice, holy, acceptable to God, *which is* your reasonable service" (Rom. 12:1). This verse is difficult to translate correctly. The word rendered "service" is the Greek *latreia*, which is more of liturgical offering than a mere act of service. Thomas Cranmer, the Anglican reformer, captured the verse well in the context of his eucharistic prayer: "And here we offer and present unto thee, O Lord, our selves, our souls and bodies, to be a reasonable, holy, and living sacrifice unto thee."

This is thanksgiving in which the whole of the self is given. It properly recognizes the dynamic of what is taking place in the Holy Eucharist. In St. John Chrysostom's words, the priest or deacon elevates the Holy Body and Blood of Christ and says, "Thine own of Thine own we offer unto Thee, on behalf of all and for all." This phrase gathers everything we have received (which constitutes the whole of creation) and offers it as the sacrifice of thanksgiving.

This eucharistic understanding extends far beyond the seeming confines of the Divine Liturgy (which truly has no confines). This is the liturgy of our existence and the expression of the life for which we were and are created. The giving of thanks is, properly, an act of vulnerability, an expression of humility. For this reason the language of the liturgy is suffused with expressions of our unworthiness and emptiness. This is not an attempt to accuse ourselves of evil or to deny the essential goodness of our existence. Rather, it is the voice of our contingent being, the confession that our life is a gift for which we can claim no authorship. It is the deepest and most eloquent expression of the nature of our existence.

Saint Paul offers what is for many a scandalous commandment, to give thanks "always and for all things" (Eph. 5:20). I have written about this statement many times through the years and always received troubled questions in return. "How can I give thanks for evil or tragic things that happen?" The questions, while honest, point to a fundamental misunderstanding of the nature of thanksgiving.

In our common, everyday life, we tend to offer thanks when something pleasant or kind has been done for us. This ingrains an attitude in which the giving of thanks becomes a kind of payment. It is an action that requires no belief in God but merely a performance of cultural politeness. In a culture driven by consumerism, the giving of thanks easily degenerates into a form of exchange, an expression of our pleasure. This differs from the greater expression of thanksgiving in the Scriptures.

Two examples of thanksgiving in the Scriptures provide a vision of this greater expression. The first can be found in the story of the three youths in the fiery furnace. There, three young men have been unjustly condemned to death in a terrible fiery furnace. Miraculously, they stand unharmed in the midst of the flames. In the fullest account of their trial, part of which is found only in the Septuagint version of the Book of Daniel, we hear them offer a hymn of praise and thanksgiving while standing in the flames. Only at the very end of this great hymn do they mention their deliverance:

"Blessed art thou, O Lord, God of our fathers,
  and to be praised and highly exalted for ever;
And blessed is thy glorious, holy name
  and to be highly praised and highly exalted for ever;
Blessed art thou in the temple of thy holy glory
  and to be extolled and highly glorified for ever." (Dan. 3:52, RSV)

This verse is followed by thirty-six verses in which every element of creation is exhorted to bless the Lord. Finally the song concludes:

"Bless the Lord, Hananiah, Azariah, and Mishael,
  sing praise to him and highly exalt him for ever;
for he has rescued us from Hades and saved us from the hand of death,
  and delivered us from the midst of the burning fiery furnace;
  from the midst of the fire he has delivered us.
Give thanks to the Lord, for he is good,
  for his mercy endures for ever.
Bless him, all who worship the Lord, the God of gods,
  sing praise to him and give thanks to him,
  for his mercy endures for ever." (Dan. 3:88–90, RSV)

Their offering in the midst of the furnace is one of the most sublime eucharistic moments to be found anywhere.[39] It is as

---

39 I remind readers that "eucharist" comes from the Greek word for "thanksgiving."

though, standing in the flames, they are directing all of creation like an orchestra, calling forth the sound of its praise to the God of all. This eucharistic offering is the priestly offering, the role intended for Adam in Paradise. As the youths take up this role, the fiery furnace is itself transformed. On the one hand, its flames can be seen as the flames of hell, the terrible image of human suffering. However, in this priestly context, the furnace becomes Eden, the center of the world and the place from which all praise arises.

There is a similar transformation in a second example of thanksgiving. That one is also a hymn but one offered by Jonah from the "belly of the whale."

I cried out to the LORD because of my affliction,
And He answered me.
Out of the belly of Sheol I cried,
And You heard my voice.
For You cast me into the deep,
Into the heart of the seas,
And the floods surrounded me;
All Your billows and Your waves passed over me.
Then I said, "I have been cast out of Your sight;
Yet I will look again toward Your holy temple."
. . .
Yet You have brought up my life from the pit, O LORD,
   my God.
When my soul fainted within me, I remembered the
   LORD;
And my prayer went *up* to You,

Into Your holy temple.

. . .

But I will sacrifice to You
With the voice of thanksgiving;
I will pay what I have vowed.
Salvation *is* of the LORD. (Jonah 2:2–9)

Jonah's "hell" (the belly of the whale) is also his deliverance. He has been cast overboard by his sailing companions in order, as he instructs them, that the storm raging around them may be calmed. He describes the belly of the beast as "Sheol," but recognizes in this an answer to prayer. He cries out to God, and God hears him. His hymn of praise concludes with the "voice of thanksgiving." Of particular note, however, is the verse that follows this hymn: "So the LORD spoke to the fish, and it vomited Jonah onto dry land."

This account of Jonah's safe recovery occurs *after* his hymn of praise. In our consumer-driven world, his hymn would only make sense if he sang it after he reached dry land. Indeed, anyone would gladly kiss the ground and shout for joy after that hideous journey's end. But Jonah sings his song from within the fish. Like the three young men in Daniel's account, Jonah has changed the belly of a fish into paradise itself. His song of thanksgiving is a eucharistic action, the fulfillment of our priestly vocation.

Both stories point to the right understanding of thanksgiving. It is the proper note of our relationship with God. Despite all circumstances, and even in the midst of the worst of circumstances, thanksgiving is the assertion of the fundamental role of our very existence. We were created to give thanks to God, not as payment in exchange for things we enjoy, but because of who and what we are: the priests of all creation. Thanksgiving is the active voice of humility, the recognition that our existence and all that we do is the gift of God. The giving of thanks is not just a response to a pleasing outcome, but *the most profound acknowledgment of who God is in all things and at all times.*

It was a commonplace in the Fathers to note a cycle between pain and pleasure (*odune* and *hedone* in Greek). We flee one and seek the other. However, when this cycle rules our life, we begin a spiral toward death. Many good things require that we reach them through bearing some amount of pain. Learning to do the hard thing rather than the thing that gives us pleasure is fundamental to a healthy existence. In the life of the Church, every feast is preceded by fasting. The greater the feast, the greater the fast.

To a degree, the practice of humility is a fast. That we are frequently confronted by shame, particularly in its rather mild healthy form, is an unavoidable fact of life. If shame is the gateway or master emotion, then all emotional encounters will involve some amount of shame. This reality is generally outside our cultural vocabulary. We may describe an encounter as "awkward" or "stumbling" because we do not see the awkwardness and the stumbling as our discomfort with the shame involved. The rules that once governed polite discourse were largely efforts to manage and rein in the misuse of shame in our intercourse with others. Such niceties have largely disappeared today, replaced either by an unfettered use of shame to overpower opponents or by the shame-driven conversations of politically correct speech.

Humility represents an effort to step back from the precipice of a Hobbesian world of constant conflict. Frequently, Christians are drawn into that world of conflict by imagining that the Faith is somehow locked in a war of ideas. The world of argument, of charge and countercharge, is rooted in the false belief that victory belongs to those who master the tools of violence (in all its forms). Humility, however, belongs to the world of the Cross. It is the "mind of Christ" enjoined on us in Philippians. Humility, the bearing of our "little shame," is an affirmation that victory belongs to the Crucified and has already been accomplished in Him.

That same victory offers the song of thanksgiving always and everywhere, for it is the last word of creation to its Creator, the song of goodness to the Good. The history of the world is a tale of scars. Every tribe across the globe has at some point been vilified, hated, and mocked. Oppression is a common human experience as we take turns giving to others what we have received. Indeed, the wounds of shame have such an enduring effect in our lives that we give to others the fruit of wounds whose reception long predates any living memory. As a recent bestseller reminds us, "The body keeps score."[40] The Christian Faith believes, however, that the score was settled long ago, making it possible for us to forgive all debts and to join in the song of thanksgiving.

As Christ and His disciples left the Upper Room and the Passover meal, the Gospels record that they sang a psalm on the way to the Garden of Gethsemane. Traditionally, that psalm

---

40 Bessel van der Kolk, *The Body Keeps Score: Brain, Mind, and Body in the Healing of Trauma* (Penguin, 2014).

would have been Psalm 118, the last of the Passover Psalms. In Orthodox usage, it is known as the "Polyeleios," the "many mercies," on account of its refrain, "For His mercy endures forever." It is one of the great hymns of thanksgiving. Like Jonah or the Three Young Men, Christ led His disciples in a hymn of thanksgiving *before* the moment of deliverance. This is the ultimate act of humility, the patient bearing of a little shame. It is in learning to sing such songs everywhere and at all times that the victory of the Cross becomes manifest within the depths of our souls.

The vision of our final healing is given in a few words by St. Paul: "But we all, with unveiled face, beholding as in a mirror the glory of the Lord, are being transformed into the same image from glory to glory, just as by the Spirit of the Lord" (2 Cor. 3:18).

It is the utter humility of God that reveals His face to us. "I did not hide My face from shame and spitting" (Is. 50:6). It is our own humility that allows us to behold His face in the mirror of the soul. When His humility is revealed in that most intimate and holy place, we see that the image of the true self is nothing other than the very image of God. In anticipation of that joy, we give thanks.

CHAPTER TEN

Going Forward: Some Last Thoughts

R ECENTLY, I READ A NEWSPAPER HEADLINE: "We will get justice." In the relentless cycle of the daily news, the report was of the discovery of the body of a young woman who had been murdered. The words quoted in the headline seemed a completely appropriate response by the law officer in charge of the investigation. His words doubtless echoed the sentiments of everyone who knew the young woman. The desire for justice is primal and among the earliest thoughts of our childhood. But what is justice?

Essentially, justice is a desire for things to be fair or even. A young child noticing an inequity will quickly announce, "It's not fair!" One person's gain often comes at the price of another's loss. This instinct for justice never disappears. A crime such as murder provokes this response at the deepest level. One person has gained something he desired (however perversely) at the expense of another's life. We demand retribution (meaning literally the "restoration of value"). It is the instinct behind the *lex talionis* ("An eye for an eye and a tooth for a tooth").

But such justice never seems to satisfy—*it is never enough*. A human life has been destroyed. Punishing the killer does not restore value—it does not bring anyone back from the dead. It is, sadly, only a fulfillment of the maxim, "An eye for an eye and the whole world's blind." Imagine the tragic case of one brother killing another. The family has lost an irreplaceable son. Justice within the law demands the loss of yet another son. There can be no making even in such a plight, only the abyss of grief. And when this occurs between two families, after "justice" is achieved, the result will be two grieving mothers. Things are now in balance, but it is a balance of emptiness and the abyss.

Justice, the desire for fairness, is both primal—rooted deep within our psyche—and also fraught with complex ironies that cause layer on layer of sin and darkness. One of those layers is envy, the desire for someone else to "get what's coming to them." Because fairness is almost always illusory, the envy that it provokes can be radically incommensurate. An angry politician a few years back denounced protestors and called for their arrests, saying, "Ruin the rest of their lives!" That is envy, an angry demand for some infinite justice. It is also evil.

Beneath the desire for justice, the anger, the envy, is the yet more primal emotion of shame. We have not simply lost the object of our desire (a child, a job, a political campaign). The loss is shaming—we feel that we have somehow been diminished, that our life has now been devalued and made smaller. What is at stake in shame is "who I am." We find loss associated with this deepest of instincts to be largely unbearable. We have lost face.

This takes us to some of the core emotions surrounding

forgiveness and points to why we find it so difficult to achieve on our own. It also points to the only way forward: "The way of shame is the way of the Lord," in the words of St. Sophrony.

The heart of the Christian gospel is the story of a God who, in an act of supreme self-emptying, humbled Himself to the point of bearing our shame. It is the ultimate loss of face. His crucifixion was utterly unfair and unjust. He is the one true Innocent who *willingly* endures a death reserved for the most shameful criminals. And it is this very path of self-emptying that He offers to us as the way of salvation. This way of salvation is not the extrinsic description of salvation found in contemporary Christianity. Salvation is the full union of our lives with the life of Christ. The shame and self-emptying of the Cross are the content of the commandment, "take up the cross, and follow Me" (Mark 10:21).

The daily expression of this self-emptying bearing of shame is spelled out in other commandments: forgive your enemies, do good to those who hate you, give without expecting in return, rejoice in your sufferings, and so forth. All these involve the loss of face. All these feel, on one level, like a diminishment of our lives.

The path of forgiveness, of love toward those who hate us, of unrequited generosity and thanksgiving for all things, represents a decision to step away from the protected life of the guarded self. It accepts injustice toward the self, the loss of what is rightfully due, and the giving of what is neither deserved nor merited. None of this would be possible for us apart from the example of Christ and our mystical union with Him.

It seems to me that we have acquired the spiritual habit of

making our salvation an abstraction. We speak of being "crucified with Christ" and of being "baptized into His death"—
language that holds a prominent place in the lexicon of the
New Testament. But we tend to treat these as happening in a
manner somehow distinct from our experience. Neither crucifixion nor death should have an association with things that
seem pleasant. Christ Himself constantly makes reference to
very unpleasant things: forgiving injustice toward the self, the
loss of what is rightfully due, giving what is neither deserved
nor merited, and so forth. These are all things that we seem to
loathe instinctively. The shame we encounter through such acts
of self-emptying is invariably painful. But this is the gospel. We
take it on *in union with Christ.*

It is in this vein that St. Sophrony speaks from within the
Tradition, saying that we must learn to "bear a little shame."
There is much that must be said in this regard. First, bearing
shame can only be *voluntary.* Involuntary shaming is always
toxic and leaves deep wounds. The experience of such wounds
surrounds the entire experience of forgiveness, underlying the
pain associated with it. The moral use of a commandment,
"You *must* forgive," can inadvertently become another tool in
the hands of others to drive the pain and burden of shame ever
deeper. There is a "time for every purpose under heaven," Eccle-
siastes tells us. The timing of the Cross was clearly an issue for
Christ Himself. In like manner, our own voluntary actions in
union with Him have their own time. We go forward as grace
makes it possible.

We must, first and foremost, understand that the bearing
of shame is not only voluntary but also something we can only

do *a little at a time.* Only Christ dies for the sins of the whole world. It is indeed possible that great saints unite themselves utterly and completely in that shame-bearing self-emptying entrance into Hades. But they did not start at that point. It is the gift of God and a work of grace operating over a lifetime.

We must, in the words of the elder, learn to "bear a *little* shame." By the same token, we learn to practice a *little* forgiveness. This is not an abandonment of the commandment of Christ but rather a sober reflection of precisely the truth of what forgiveness entails. Our voluntary bearing of that little shame unites us with Christ, who took the whole of all shame on Himself and said, "Father, forgive them."

Lastly, bearing shame requires *safety.* Shame involves deep vulnerability. We feel exposed and naked—even, in instances of toxic shame, abused and raped. Like victims of trauma, we can only visit the memories of such things when we are assured that we are not walking again into fresh abuse. Christ dwelt "in the bosom of the Father." The Father never abandoned Him (*pace* those who misunderstand His words on the Cross).[41] In the Garden of Gethsemane, Christ reckons the full cost of His self-emptying, but He does so in utter communion and knowledge of the Father. He goes to the Cross "for the joy set before Him . . . despising the shame" (Heb. 12:2).

In our communion with Christ and in the bosom of the Church, it is possible to know the safety sufficient for forgiveness and the shame it entails. But, again, it must be voluntary,

---

41 See Eugenia Scarvelis Constantinou's *The Crucifixion of the King of Glory: The Amazing History and Sublime Mystery of the Passion* (Chesterton, IN: Ancient Faith Publishing, 2022), 332.

resulting from our acceptance of Christ's Cross, in union with His own joyful acceptance, and not through some moral compulsion. One enemy at a time, we make our way into the love of God, learning step by step the joyful way of Christ's self-emptying.

Saint John of the Ladder wrote, "You cannot escape shame except by shame." It is one of the great paradoxes of the Faith, a paradox resolved only in the Cross of Christ. I pray that the reflections in this book will allow you to take small steps in this journey, that God will grant you loving and supportive friends in this struggle, and that, at last, we may all behold Christ face to face, without shame or fear, and find the mystery of wholeness made manifest in our lives.

Recommended Reading

Bradshaw, John. *Healing the Shame that Binds You.* Deerfield Beach, FL: Health Communications, Inc., 2010.

Burgo, Joseph. *Shame.* New York: St. Martin's Press, 2018.

Frank, Adam J., and Elizabeth Willson. *A Silvan Tomkins Handbook: Foundations for Affect Theory.* University of Minnesota Press, 2020.

Kaufman, Gershen. *The Psychology of Shame: Theory and Treatment of Shame-Based Syndromes.* New York: Springer Publishing, 1996.

Kaufman, Gershen. *Shame: The Power of Caring.* Shenkman Books, 1992.

Nathanson, Donald. *The Many Faces of Shame.* Guilford Press, 1987.

Potter-Efron, Ronald, and Patricia Potter-Efron. *Letting Go of Shame: Understanding How Shame Affects Your Life.* Hazelden, 1989.

Van der Kolk, Bessel A. *The Body Keeps the Score: Brain, Mind, and Body in the Healing of Trauma.* New York: Penguin Books, 2015.

F R. STEPHEN FREEMAN is an archpriest in the Orthodox
Church in America and is Pastor Emeritus of St. Anne
Orthodox Church in Oak Ridge, Tennessee. He was educated
at Furman University, Seabury-Western Theological Semi-
nary, and Duke University. He is the author of the popular blog
Glory to God for All Things and of the weekly podcast *Glory to
God* on Ancient Faith Radio, as well as the book *Everywhere
Present: Christianity in a One-Storey Universe* (Ancient Faith
Publishing, 2010). Fr. Stephen is a popular speaker at confer-
ences, colleges, and parishes across the country. His work has
been widely translated and published in Europe and Russia.

We hope you have enjoyed and benefited from this book. Your financial support makes it possible to continue our non-profit ministry both in print and online. Because the proceeds from our book sales only partially cover the costs of operating **Ancient Faith Publishing** and **Ancient Faith Radio**, we greatly appreciate the generosity of our readers and listeners. Donations are tax deductible and can be made at **www.ancientfaith.com**.

To view our other publications,
please visit our website: **store.ancientfaith.com**

 **ANCIENT FAITH RADIO**

Bringing you Orthodox Christian music, readings,
prayers, teaching, and podcasts 24 hours a day since 2004 at
www.ancientfaith.com

Ingram Content Group UK Ltd.
Milton Keynes UK
UKHW011313040423
419632UK00004B/163